THE IN-BETWEEN YEARS

A FORMER NUN'S STORY OF LIFE IN A CONVENT

THE IN-BETWEEN YEARS

A FORMER NUN'S STORY OF LIFE IN A CONVENT

BY

MARY ZENCHOFF

> *For twenty-four years, Mary lived in a convent. She endured conditions that most of us never realized existed. Near-starvation, social deprivation, and impossible work assignments prevailed while Mary worked and prayed, and struggled to understand whether this was the life Jesus and God meant for her.*

Bookstand Publishing

www.bookstandpublishing.com

Published by
Bookstand Publishing
Morgan Hill, CA 95037
4551_3

ISBN 978-1-63498-562-8

Library of Congress Control Number: 2017952183

Printed in the United States of America

DEDICATION

This book is dedicated to my beloved husband, Phil, whose companionship, invaluable help, steadfast encouragement, and eternal love made everything possible.

SPECIAL NOTE

Suddenly, with no warning and of unknown cause, on the morning of August 22, 2016, Mary passed away. At that time, this book was in the hands of her friend and editor, in the middle of its final edit.

With members of Mary's family, I discussed the matter of the book and the question of what to do with it. The majority agreed that *The In-Between Years* remains Mary's greatest work, the work to which she dedicated much of her energy for the last years of her life and of which she felt most proud. It must be published.

So it is that, sandwiched between other projects, editor Cybele Sieradzki prepared *The In-Between Years* for publication. We are most grateful for her knowledgeable and efficient effort. Mary would be most pleased.

Phil Zenchoff
July 5, 2017

FOREWORD

I was eighteen years old when I entered the convent. Twenty-four years later I left. I was ecstatic when I entered, and even more ecstatic when I closed the door behind me.

This is the story of those in-between years, the years when I ate the left-over fish that the seminarians refused, and had no choice in where I would teach, and loved the kids, and wept when I was transferred to another school.

It is the tale of going to a therapist for professional help in dealing with convent life, and being told that the therapist had fallen in love with a priest and needed advice for a broken heart from me, who hadn't had a date in fifteen years.

It is the story of striking out on my own and finally earning my own money, and visiting some old sisters' retirement homes and realizing that, if I stayed in the convent—as dear as the old sisters were—someday, I would be caught in a trap of my own making.

It is the story of finally knowing when the time had come for me to leave the convent, free at last.

So there were the beginning years, when I found out what it was all about and wondered and wondered if I had made the right decisions, and finally there was the freedom of the ending years that began when I was forty-two years old.

The title of this book is *The In-Between Years*. It is the story of the years that were more astounding and strange than anything else that has ever happened to me.

TABLE OF CONTENTS

PROLOGUE

There is a background to any story about convent life. That background is the world of first communions and rosary beads and long Masses during which, as a young girl, she wiggled and was gently corrected by parents or sisters until she returned to her prayer books with the brightly colored holy cards that were supposed to focus her attention again. It is the world that led her to think that she could follow the strict rules of monastic orders, cut her hair and wear a habit that symbolized her dedication to God. It is the world that gave her a kind of confused peace that she could not explain to those who were not in a monastic order.

It is a world that is part of every Catholic woman, whether or not she enters a convent. It is a world in which God is looked to for help and solace in the midst of trials and troubles in married life and in single life. It is a world in which the joys and happiness of common occurrences are shared with God as much as they are with friends. There is no escape from that world nor does she want to escape. She knows that the mysteries that she never understood when she was a child are still a world of confusion to her, but something deep inside her knows that she cannot live without those mysteries and that world.

If she is in the convent she tries to be obedient to its rules unless and until she makes her own rules for her life. Even then her own rules have remnants of the convent rules, because they are what she believes in and is comfortable with. Outsiders never understand what is going on with her. But she knows.

If she leaves the convent she takes parts of it with her because she cannot live without those truths that she lived by for months or years. Something unique is going on and, usually, only other Catholics can understand the reality of it. She does not try to explain why she entered or why she stayed, or even why she left. It is a world apart.

That is why a prologue is necessary and why a prologue is useless. Catholics write their own prologues. Non-Catholics often give up trying to fathom the whole thing. They say, "You didn't say anything!" and she answers, "I know. It cannot be put into words." She goes back to the convent or her marriage or single life knowing that she did her best to explain everything. She is not upset if it is never understood.

THE TRUNK: A SYMBOL OF BOTH LEAVING AND ARRIVING

The trunk, big and black with brass locks and leather handles, was in a corner of our old-fashioned dining room. The trunk waited for the clothing and other things I would take with me to the convent when I became a novice. But, instead of packing anything in it, my parents had nightly arguments about allowing me to enter the convent, usually when they thought I was asleep.

My father's aunt had been in the convent for many years. He acted as though I would be carrying on a hallowed family tradition when I "took the veil," as people termed it in those days. My mother sighed whenever my father brought up the subject and said, "She's too young. She's only eighteen years old."

So, as a result of their indecision, the trunk remained empty. Without the trunk full of my wonderful new clothing, sending my application to the superiors at the Mother house was useless. I felt like screaming. Sometimes I sneaked around when my mother was out shopping, just to peer at the trunk, as if it were a shrine of some kind.

This is where my new clothes will be kept, I promised myself as I dreamed of the moment when I would be at the Motherhouse along with my trunk.

As the September entrance day approached, my mother suddenly stopped saying anything, as if she knew she had lost the battle. When I saw her quietly slip out the door for early Mass, I wondered if she still prayed that I would change my mind. Maybe she just hoped that she could bear my leaving home.

My father kept his feelings to himself, once he saw that things were going his way. A few weeks before my entrance day, he called me over to his desk, took out his checkbook and showed me how much money was in the family account.

"I saved some of this for your college education," he said hesitantly, as if he should not even mention money to someone who was about to reject possession of any riches at all. Somehow, I didn't understand what he was trying to say to me. I had never found it easy to talk to him, especially now. I just smiled hesitantly, and patted the checkbook, as if it were a person who could absorb gratitude.

And my sister! A lot of competition always had swirled between us. Now she tried to be part of my departure in a sharing kind of way. She defended me once or twice when I opposed some of my father's bossiness, something she had never done before.

Once, I overheard her whisper to one of her girlfriends, "It will be like a funeral when Mary is gone." I wondered if she really meant it.

Then there was my little brother, with his wild but endearing ways. How could I ever leave him? He was comical in the way that small boys are, snatching up my new black veil from the corner by the trunk and prancing around the living room. My precious veil fluttered like a cloud and he ran from the room as I shouted after him and both of us enjoyed the fun of it all.

The day my parents finally sat down with me and told me that they were willing to let me "try out" the convent life, I felt joyous. I looked at them lovingly, and tried to tell them how much I would miss them, but my mother's face crumbled as though she were going to cry, so I said nothing to them.

Maybe later, I promised myself, and just hugged them.

There was so much to think about. Once my parents finally agreed that I could enter the convent, I began to worry over the atomic bomb. It was 1952 and the newspapers were full of the progress of brilliant scientists in Moscow. Rumors of their secret plots had burgeoned for months. Were they ready to drop atomic bombs on our people? What would happen to my blissful dreams if they succeeded?

All I really thought about were my own plans. I pictured myself heroically stumbling over piles of radioactive rubble, frantically trying to reach the Motherhouse, where I pleaded with the Mother Superior to open the cloister gates to me. What about my mother and father, my sister and little brother? Why wasn't I more concerned for them? "Don't focus on anything else except being in the convent," I whispered to myself. "God will take care of them."

Two weeks before my entrance day, my parents and I received an invitation to come to the local convent to take care of some last-minute details. A sister ushered us into a crowded room, where we joined a long line of chattering teen-age girls and their edgy parents. Among the crowd, I recognized a girl whom I had never liked. Usually, I avoided her whenever I entered the school lunchroom.

"Hi, Molly," I said. "What are you doing here?"

To my annoyance, she answered, with a smirk, "I'm entering the convent. Too bad you got here after I did. I'll always be ahead of you in rank."

I knew what rank meant. My father had been in the army. Rank meant that Molly would be ahead of me for everything, the first to get her mail, the first to go to meals, the first of anything at all. She would be at the head of the line no matter how long the line was, and all because my mother had been slow putting on her hat when we should have hurried to catch the bus. Was this the way life in the convent was going to be? I wanted to shove Molly out of the way, but a hawk-eyed nun standing in the front of the room was watching me. I gave Molly what I hoped was a humble smile, befitting a future nun. Maybe I could find some sneaky way to get even with her for acting so high-and-mighty. God didn't owe me anything for leaving home to follow Him, but did I really have to be holy before I even had the veil on my head?

My mother had agreed earlier that she would sign some kind of a required legal document for the convent; she poked me.

"That nun with the name tag is waiting for us," she said nervously. I squinted and managed to read the tag.

"That's Mother Josepha," I said shyly. "She's in charge of all the new sisters like me."

My mother hurried up to the grim-faced owner of the badge, glanced at a single-page document, and signed on the line to which the unsmiling Mother Josepha pointed.

"Any money that your daughter may earn while she is in the convent will belong to the Motherhouse," Mother Josepha announced pompously, as though my mother were too naive to understand what the document stated. My mother nodded in agreement, but her lips were tight, the way they looked when she secretly wanted to slap someone. My father remained uncharacteristically silent. They both began looking at the ceiling, the walls and each other as though it would ease their nerves if they didn't look directly at me.

Finally, I caught my father's eye.

Maybe he doesn't know how to tell me that he will miss me, I thought hopefully. I had always been the one who told him, "No," when I didn't want to do something. My knees might tremble, but I still whispered a firm refusal whenever I mustered up the courage to oppose him. I wondered sometimes how I would manage to be obedient to a superior in the convent.

You will have to pray a lot, I told myself. Maybe I would never learn to obey and they would order me to leave the convent immediately. Something in me wondered if I was entering the convent just to show my father one last time that I was in charge of my own life.

My mother nudged me because Mother Josepha was obviously waiting for something.

"Dad," I said, "Mother Josepha is waiting for the dowry." My dignified father suddenly looked awkward and handed her a thin envelope marked "Dowry." He was giving her a $100 check, required by the instructions sent to my home a few weeks before. I was like the bartered bride from medieval times when the father paid tribute to the patriarch of a powerful family, only it was not like giving a cache of priceless jewels or a castle for the king's defense in case of attack. It was my father's hard-earned money, and it was being given to the convent. What a satisfying moment. I felt like a bride already. Mother Josepha gave them a cramped smile and motioned to the next set of parents to approach.

I wonder if she ever heard of saying, 'thank you,' or does she just take it for granted when someone gives money to her, I thought angrily. Already I didn't like her and my life in the convent hadn't really begun.

The whole day was breathtaking for me until I saw how sad my parents looked. I loved them so much. They still didn't grasp why I had to leave them. Maybe later on they would, but that was not the day. So I politely restrained my emotions until I could get home, call my girlfriends, and shout my exuberant reaction to signing away my life. It was a red-letter day for me, but not for my parents.

FILLING THE TRUNK

Every evening, I called my closest friend, Claire. We chattered like little magpies for hours on end, much to the distress of our parents. They preferred that we talk about movie stars, or old boyfriends, instead of counting the days until we entered the convent. We took off together on special trips to huge stores in Manhattan where rows of black clothing were displayed for girls like us. Black dresses, black blouses, black capes. We touched them all with reverence. We were in our new world.

It was like the trip a bride-to-be takes to the bridal shop. She picks out all the negligees and beautiful underwear and other luxurious articles that are connected with her new life. But the objects that we bought to put into our big black trunks were things like white cotton bloomers (the old lady style) or long black lisle stockings so they would last forever, or baggy white nightgowns with long sleeves and high necks.

Once, when our entrance day was only a few weeks away, I trailed a solemn-faced salesman who had ignored me for several minutes as I wandered through that cavernous store, daydreaming about my future. Finally I caught his eye, picked up a black cape, and said shyly, "Can I try this on?" He nodded and I grinned excitedly at myself in the narrow mirror, preening a bit while he was occupied with another customer. I wondered later if he shook his head sadly when he told his wife about me that evening, especially if they had daughters. Maybe his wife said, "At least her mother will know where she is at night," and the husband groaned at her little joke.

When we were finally finished, Claire and I picked up our bundles and hurried home, chattering all the way.

"We'll be wearing these clothes," we chortled to each other, rejoicing in our freedom to be excited without worrying about our parents. The clothes were signs of our new future. Even seeing my mother's anxious face later, as she folded the old-fashioned garments and put them carefully into my trunk, did not drain my joy. I felt sorry for my parents because I loved them dearly. I told my religious superiors, "God comes first." But in the end, it was really myself that I loved the most.

ENTRANCE DAY, AT LAST

I was so excited on entrance day. As soon as my next-door neighbor opened her door to pick up her newspaper, I shouted loudly, "I'm entering the convent today, Mrs. Devine."

She smiled kindly at me and said what so many people would say for the rest of my life, "Well, say a prayer for me, dear," like I were a plaster saint already enshrined in the local church.

I agreed solemnly, as though I were making some kind of religious vow, and gave her a hug that I hoped made up for all the times I had ignored her in the past when I didn't feel like having a conversation with her about her cat or her problems with the delivery boy from the grocery store.

I could hear my mother calling, "Mary! It's time to go." I closed the door of our apartment, as I welcomed the reprieve. I began to feel rather sad and nervous. I hadn't thought about how it would be to leave home for the first time in my life.

Am I making a mistake? I suddenly asked myself. It was a scary thought.

My parents hurried me out to the car where Claire and her parents were waiting. We drove together to the Motherhouse, where we got our first dose of what it would mean to be sisters. It didn't enter our teen-age minds how challenging the next two years would be. We could think only about ourselves, our girlish dreams, our trunks laden with our special clothing. We grinned at one another, and calmed our nerves with little giggles. Our parents continued chatting nervously about the Kremlin and the atomic bomb. They glanced at us every few minutes as if we might vanish if they didn't keep us in their sight.

The trip to the Motherhouse took only an hour. I sprang out of the car, thrilled to see other black-clad girls with their flimsy black veils that slipped off their heads, just like mine did. I waited for something else to happen, something momentous that would remind me of why I was really there. Perhaps a Mother Superior would call out our names and bring us forward one at a time to be introduced, or an old frail sister would speak to the group of us, saying, "I came here sixty years ago and I learned to love this life." Nothing like this occurred.

Instead the boom of the chapel bell interrupted my confused thoughts. It was time for dinner, my first meal in my new home. Food! Yes, I knew about food! I expected that it would be fattening food for a celebratory meal, a meal that would say, "Welcome. We are so glad you are here!" I grabbed Claire's hand and walked in what I hoped was a fairly dignified gait toward the huge doors of the Motherhouse. I longed to run. Once again I felt overwhelmed by the wonderful excitement that had flooded me at the beginning of the day. I was ready to start my new and beautiful life.

I had never been inside the dining area of this massive convent. The refectory, as it was formally called, was arranged to seat 150 sisters. I felt swallowed up by the mere number of tables and chairs arranged in such precise patterns. Was this the type of orderliness that I would be expected to imitate in the days to come? I was the usual slap-dash-who-cares-where-I-put–things teenager. How would I ever fit in? Maybe I should have listened to my parents and waited a few more years. By then I would have grown up a bit. But it was too late. I was being shuffled along with all the other black-robed youngsters to several long tables. The same frightened look was on each face, the "lost-soul look," as I later christened it. Claire's table was not even near mine. I suddenly felt alone.

I huddled over my plate, with its meager contents. Slabs of bologna, slices of thick bread and a dab of apple butter comprised my dinner. Large pitchers of ice-water were on each table. I was famished, but, unlike Oliver Twist, I knew I had better not ask for anything more. I glanced in Claire's direction, wishing we could talk about our feelings. She was not close enough for us to whisper even a word or two to each other. How had I ever gotten myself into this situation, I who liked boys, food and endless chatting? Would God be enough for me?

The meal was eaten in deadly silence, broken only by the drone of the sister reading the life of the saint for the day. The saint was running frantically from beheading by a pagan king who wanted her to marry his handsome son. The story did not inspire me. By the end of the meal, I was having niggling little thoughts such as, *Why am I here?* and *How do I get a nickel to make a phone call to my mother, father, brother or former arch enemy to get me out of here?*

The murmuring of the reader finally stopped. The little bell at the Mother Superior's table rang, signaling the end of the meal. I humbly followed the long line of my veiled companions. I was led down a curving stone hallway to the chapel for evening prayers. To my shock, the prayers were in Latin. Would I be praying in Latin, not just for today or tomorrow, but forever? When had I been told that I had to pray in Latin? It was such a cold, formal language, so devoid of comfort. I had always liked praying in my own little way, muttering my thoughts, as well as my complaints, to God at numerous times during the day.

At last, the final prayers for the day were over. Mother Josepha hurried us up a steep flight of stairs leading to our bedrooms. We would be sleeping in the attic, with curtains separating our beds; a tin basin with a small washcloth was placed precariously on an equally precarious table next to each bed. Thrown carelessly on a chair were a small pillow and a thin blanket. Mother Josepha pointed out some narrow closets nearby and informed us that each of us could use only one shelf for our possessions.

"And let's all remember," she added, "that there is no talking allowed in our cells. We reserve our conversations for God here."

The only thing I cared about at that moment was washing my face and going to bed. Complaints could come later when I was able to talk to Claire. We would laugh then at calling our bedrooms "cells." I felt a little wave of pride that I was so quickly catching on to convent vocabulary. It made me feel as though I really belonged.

The last thought that fluttered through my mind was a sense of happiness that at last I was here in the convent. This had been a day of highs and lows. There was a lot to get used to. It was not as easy as I had thought it would be.

RISE AND SHINE

The bell rang too early the following morning for me to face the day with anything but a groan. I dressed frantically, pulled on my new black dress and dabbed at my eyes with a damp wash cloth that I left in my little metal basin the night before when the last silence bell rang. My veil was hopelessly askew, my hair half-combed. I rushed down the steep stairs to the chapel, feeling untidy. My shoes clattered on the uncarpeted steps and earned me my first glance of kindly-disapproval from the older sisters who were already in their chapel seats, gazing at the altar piously. They had learned how to get from one floor to another without leaving even a whisper of sound. They could dress without a mirror. They looked beautiful the way I hoped to look someday. They were what I wanted to become.

The first order of the day, as soon as I had been shuttled along with my black-robed companions into our proper places, was to sit quietly and meditate for a half-hour. I kicked my wooden kneeler before I even opened my prayer book. I wished someone I knew was sitting near me, to give me a forgiving smile. But everyone seemed focused on their prayers.

My head bounced awkwardly on my chest as I struggled to stay awake.

Is this the only kind of meditation that I can manage? I asked myself. *I wonder if anyone is watching me.*

Mother Josepha, the mistress of novices, rang a little bell that was like a wake-up call. I scrambled to my feet and rubbed my eyes to make sure I was awake. It was time for the next layer of prayers for the day.

I stood at attention, clutched my prayer book and frantically turned the pages as I tried to find the right psalm. I glanced at Claire, who stood in the row opposite me. She looked so tired.

Oh, Claire, I thought. *What have we done?*

I wondered if she was ranking her decision, as "good, bad or doesn't fall into any known category as yet." I ached to talk to her. Maybe after breakfast Mother Josepha would give us a little time to talk. It might make us feel at home in this strange, silent place into which we had stumbled with such innocent anticipation.

The rise and fall of rhythmic Latin phrases began to soothe me. The English translation was in the column next to the Latin, so I could understand what we were chanting. For the next half-hour, I mumbled psalms written by King David many centuries ago when he was not busy eyeing someone else's wife. I mangled the endless phrases of the King's apologies to God once David had been forced into acknowledging his transgressions for future generations to cluck over. In my still-childish heart, I felt that he should have apologized to me for making such embarrassing descriptions of his sexy sins. I was an inexperienced teen-ager, not eager to be exposed to life in the tents of a long-ago desert king in Israel, especially when I was in a convent chapel. In the old days, Claire and I would have poked each other and turned down the edges of the pages we wanted to go back to later. Now I prayed, but I really wanted to giggle.

After an hour of tedious prayers passed, it was time for something that I was familiar with, namely the Holy Mass. Why hadn't I realized how many prayers there would be in this life? I felt overwhelmed. When the Mass was finally over, I followed my now-familiar compatriots to the refectory for what I hoped would be a more palatable breakfast than last night's dinner had been.

I hurried so I could catch up to my old friend, Claire. Maybe I could squeeze into the same "table for ten" where I had been seated last night. Ah, but seating at meals, unfortunately for Claire and me, was prearranged by the dreaded rank to which I had been already assigned when I was in the local convent waiting to meet Mother Josepha, the Superior for all the new members. Molly, the snippy girl who explained the meaning of rank to me then, was now one of my table companions. For the first time I realized that, in the future, I would not choose freely with whom I would eat. It was a rude awakening. A small thing, perhaps, but it meant something.

I ate a crusty roll and a thin slab of liverwurst, relieved by the semi-decent meal. Maybe last night's meager supper was a mistake and the cook had been reminded to be more careful in the future. I listened, with as much attention as I could muster, to a page or two from the rule book by which I would be living for the rest of my life. It did not sound difficult. Relief began to sweep over me. Maybe this was really the life for me. I felt suddenly virtuous and almost sisterly. I shot a quick glance at Claire who was sitting at the next table and spotted a little smile on her face. Maybe the two of us would prove all the nay-sayers wrong.

I told myself, *Someday, Claire and I will become wrinkled old ladies, in our beautiful white habits. We will be the ones greeting new groups of young girls in their black dresses and their somber veils, telling them by our smiles and our love that all will be well.* Even at this early stage in my convent career, I liked casting myself in the superior role of guiding others.

Mother Superior's little bell rang. Claire and I, as a cohesive unit, moved together toward the chapel, which alarmed me because I had not realized I would have to pray again so soon. We chanted the next section of prayers while we stood. I was able to remain upright, swaying only occasionally from weariness. I wished that my parents could see me praying in Latin. It would have made my father proud.

He would say to my mother, "You see, I was right all along. She is doing just fine." And my mother would clench her fists and stare at the altar.

In my former life, as I quickly learned to describe the years before I marched off to the convent, both Claire and I could stay up any number of hours man-hunting in various Manhattan haunts where we thought some suitable young fellow might have wandered looking for someone such as Claire or me. The adrenaline required for such an activity was fueled by the excitement of the chase.

There is nothing exciting about my life anymore, I thought mournfully as the prayers ended. *Only a dull breakfast and a reader droning on and on. Maybe things will get better when I get to know people.*

I HAVE SOME QUALMS

One of the biggest challenges in adjustment to convent life was the fact that most of my day was spent in silence. I always was a chatterbox. This character flaw, already pointed out to me several times by Mother Josepha, made it close to impossible to find out how my friends felt about our new life. I had so many questions.

'Do you really like it here?' and 'Is this what you expected the convent to be like?' were two of my most pressing questions.

Suppose I told someone how much I hated to pray in Latin and she stared at me and said, "It's the best part of my day"?

Or what if I asked someone else how long she thought she could manage to stay, and she smiled piously and said, "I want to stay here forever."

Would I be embarrassed that I had even asked? Who could I trust with my feelings?

If only I could talk and talk about how I felt about the whole situation. That was what I did when my older sister at home bossed me around too much, or when I was convinced that I was going to fail geometry and never graduate from high school. These were grave concerns when I was eighteen years old and living at home, where I couldn't be thrown out by my parents even if they were "sick and tired" of my shenanigans and had come to the last slivers of their patience. But in the end my parents were there when I needed someone to listen to me. Now I was alone.

I wanted to give my opinion on the endless prayers or on the food that I would surreptitiously slip to the family cat if I still lived at home, but the thought of making a comment to anyone scared me.

Someone might tell Mother Josepha that I had trouble adjusting to convent life.

Would she glare at me and say in her high pitched voice, "Sister Mary, do you feel beyond any doubt that you belong here?"

My immediate answer would be, "Mother Josepha, I pray every day that it will be my life forever."

But I really longed to answer angrily, "How can I know so soon? I had no idea it would be so difficult."

I wanted Mother Josepha to stop peering at me as though she thought I didn't belong. I didn't want to leave the convent. I just needed some help in evaluating my new surroundings.

If only I could whisper to Claire about my adjustment worries and find out if she felt the same way. Two of my other high-school buddies, Ann and Betty, didn't sit near me during recreation so I could only wonder what they thought. One would have to be there to understand what was really going on. I, who had been such a social-butterfly when I was living at home, was desperately lonely. I rapidly discovered that God was not enough. The old-time comfort of daily chatting and giggling with my girl-friends was gone.

Most of all, I missed my mother. Mother Josepha was hardly a substitute for her.

Claire commented one day when we had an unexpected moment together, "Mary, she doesn't understand us, and besides she is too old!"

I was rapidly getting old myself in this situation, where life consisted of examining my conscience twice a day and wondering when I would start to feel holy.

After a few weeks of silently wandering through the halls, keeping my eyes cast down, as the rule book told me to do, and speaking only when charity required it, I suddenly said to myself, "I can't live this way."

A little story I'd read about Buddha popped into my head. It described how he looked over the wall of his palace and discovered that most people were not living the life he was living.

Well, I told myself, *My friends are not clinging to the pattern I've been trying so hard to follow. I am being ridiculous in my slavish adherence to the Rule, and feel so guilty when I see how I am failing.*

My friends acted like normal human beings. They murmured in dark corners. They talked to pals at the next table in the recreation hall instead of confining their speech only to the sister next to them. A few wild ones in the group wrote messages on the plates used to cover the food that was heated up on the stove for late comers.at dinner.

"Don't eat this unless you have paid your life insurance," the bold letters proclaimed.

When the authors of such impudent sentiments were caught scrawling their innocent jokes on the convent crockery, they were reprimanded by Mother Josepha. Once in a while, she gave them a penance so they would behave themselves the next time.

It was not long until I relaxed enough to bend some of the rules myself. I still prayed. I still wanted to be a nun. But I knew nothing in this world could ever stop me from talking and having fun again. My adjustment began to "kick in." What I had not understood was that the adjustment would be cultural as well as religious.

The community of nuns that I had joined came from Ratisbon, Germany several centuries ago. It had what I called an "Achtung" outlook on how a silly little youngster like me should conform to religious rules. Without realizing some of the implications of my action, I joined an old-fashioned monastic community and then wondered why it was so strict, with such heavy emphasis on Latin chanting and ancient penances. Claire and I used to question the abundance of German names like Waltruda and Cunegunda. Some of the older sisters still called each other Schwester, the German term for Sister. They repeated the story of their long-ago migration to this country as often as they could, wanting it to be a part of our history as well. I would have been happier if, after I listened to their proud tales, I could have told them my own stories of the potato famine in Ireland or about the bravery of the patriots who suffered the bloody results of the wearing of the green. I would have watched for their fading eyes to glisten with sudden attention to those ethnic stories from my own Irish culture.

In the end, I did the only thing I could do in this bastion of German culture that I had inadvertently entered. I listened. I learned to love them for their loyalty to their roots. I even felt a small pride that I belonged to a group of sisters whose history stretched back so many centuries. These sisters were old and a little doddering, but they were real. They had reached a mellow stage in their lives, one that I yearned to reach myself.

Mother Josepha, on the other hand, decided that we needed to learn to love the austere aspects of Germanic convent life. Christmas rapidly approached. She wanted us to view the weeks before Christmas as a time of sacrifice. Claire and I whispered to each other stubbornly that being away from our parents was sacrifice enough. The struggle began. There were two protagonists: Mother Josepha's asceticism, with its devotion to suffering, and our loneliness, succored by memories of parental love. We wondered who would win, who would be happy on Christmas Day.

OUR FIRST CONVENT CHRISTMAS

Mother Josepha initiated long droning readings at breakfast from German folklore, about a mysterious spirit named the "Christkindl," who was responsible for gift-giving at Christmas in Germany. She directed us to pray for the right attitude towards giving gifts. We had to give a holy card anonymously to a nun whose name we picked out of a shuffled pack. We said prayers for her through gritted teeth. We put a makeshift Christmas card into a homemade envelope. We waited for Christmas to come.

Everything had been taken away from us. All the sweet Christmas planning was gone. The thrill of finding the right gift for a person we loved had vanished. In its place were the unfamiliar Christkindl arrangements made by Mother Josepha, the lack of human contact, the loss of the Christmas secrets we used to hug to our bosoms when we were still home. The focus now was on the birth of Christ alone. We had thought that was all we wanted but we found out that we wanted more. We wanted what we had experienced at home; we waited for the warmth we had expected to be ours in the convent, but it was not there.

The week before Christmas Day passed in a kind of nervous blur. We practiced Christmas hymns to sing at the old Sisters' home across the avenue from our huge convent. We helped to prepare the Christmas turkeys and set out red poinsettias for the altar decorations. The older sisters whispered to us that there would be no bell to awaken us for Midnight Mass. We worried that we would miss the Mass and be in trouble with Mother Josepha. There was nothing that was not beautiful, but it was not home. It was too religious for us. Where were the fun, the triumph of finding presents hidden in a closet where our parents thought we would never look? Where was the secrecy that thrilled our childish hearts? Where was the human love that we could recognize? They were absent.

On Christmas Eve we tossed half-asleep on our narrow beds, waiting for someone to signal us that it was time to go to the chapel for Midnight Mass. The sound of a lone violin startled us with its sweet tones of Silent Night, echoing through the hallway and drifting into our tiny attic sleeping quarters. Mother Josepha, in her fine white habit played the violin with the practiced hand of a true musician. Our hearts lifted. No one spoke a word. We listened to her lovely concert fading gradually as she went from floor to floor. At last we silently made our joyful way to the chapel for Midnight Mass.

Our real Christmas came the next morning when we saw our parents coming through the doors of the beautiful old stone convent. Their smiles mingled with our own. We were so glad to be able to shout Merry Christmas to them. They gave us their specially wrapped gifts, with little notes attached that we read and re-read later on. The gifts themselves, once they were opened, had to be presented to Mother Josepha who we hoped would give us permission to keep them. She did so, with a stiff smile. We were so relieved that we excused her for her harshness to us in the past. Maybe her family hadn't come to see her. We were ready to forgive her, to accept her on this loveliest of days. We thanked her shyly for last night's violin concert.

We put the little notes that our parents had written to us under our pillows that night, and hoped they would give us sweet dreams. We awoke the next morning, unexpectedly peaceful.

If you asked us six months ago, what we expected our first Christmas in the convent to be like, we would have stammered searching for the right words. Now that it was over, we knew there were no answers. There was only a sense of well-being that we were in the place where we were meant to be.

Relax, Mary, I told myself. And I did so, cheerily breaking rules, accepting old-fashioned penances, praying eagerly some days, meditating half-asleep other times, and often wanting to be a nun, but just as often wishing that I was at home. It was my life and figuring it out was a harder task than I had anticipated.

WHEN WILL I LEARN HOW TO LIVE THIS LIFE?

The humdrum daily routine settled in again after the Christmas excitement simmered down. I felt slightly anesthetized by the pain of separation from my parents and old friends, whom I saw only once a month, and the rules of silence still created havoc with my emotions. I left a little note in Claire's prayer bench in the chapel.

"Claire, we need to talk. Meet me after lunch in the laundry room, love, M."

It was a dangerous thing to do, but I was feeling desperate.

Who can live without friends? I thought to myself.

I remembered an old hymn that began, "What a friend we have in Jesus," and I wondered if He was supposed to be the only friend I had. I hoped I hadn't put myself into some kind of a box from which there was no escape. But He did something delightful, that Jesus of mine, because Claire was waiting for me that afternoon. She looked angry, but she was there.

"Are you crazy?" she hissed. "We'll both be sent home!"

We knew the laundry room was the best place to talk for a few minutes. The old-fashioned machines with their clanking parts and clouds of steam had even Schotze, the crippled sister in charge of the laundry, taking a breather every five or ten minutes. Claire and I sometimes offered to "watch the gauges" on one of the larger machines and to scream loudly if the numbers catapulted into the red zone. That was how we grabbed the few minutes of private time that we so sorely needed. Schotze understood youngsters rushing around her with tight faces, anxious because they couldn't talk to anyone except Mother Josepha without getting into trouble. Schotze slipped out the laundry door, leaving Claire and me alone.

Claire began biting her lower lip, something she always did when she was frightened.

"Mary," she blurted out." I think we'll have to follow the rules as they are. We can sneak around a little and whisper when we can manage to do so without causing a tsunami. But we aren't in boarding school. We are in the convent and we are on the way to becoming nuns together. We will have more and more friends. Just wait and see!" She gave me a little hug and hurried out of the laundry. I was left alone.

I felt abandoned, but I knew she was right. Something told me to concentrate on learning how to teach because that was what I would be doing for many years to come in this teaching community. I scooped up my books and, as fast as convent rules would permit, hurried to the class for which I was already late. But I felt more alone than I had when I wrote Claire my little note and left it in her prayer bench. If I didn't have Claire to understand me, I had only Jesus, who was not always available. He was not like my mother or my best friend at home. I had thought that He would be all things to me, but He wasn't. What was missing? Something was wrong.

WHO WILL TEACH US HOW TO TEACH?

A few weeks after Christmas, Mother Josepha herded all fifty of us into a cramped classroom for the first of many lessons in how to teach.

Somewhere, I told myself excitedly that morning, *there is a school where little children will call me "Sister." They'll go home and tell their mothers that they have a wonderful new teacher.* The knowledge that I would learn how to teach children made the dearth of good food, the strictness of the rules, and the limits of communication imposed on me more bearable.

Mother Josepha was in charge of helping us grasp the best ways to teach a vast array of elementary school subjects. We learned methodology as demanded by the Bishop, so the diplomas granted by our schools could be considered valid by the State of New York. I had no concept of the difficulty of her task. I knew only that she had the necessary skills to teach me. I really believed I would be a teacher when my lessons with her were finished. Sometimes, I wondered how successful she really was. Underneath her brusque manner, she seemed so unsure of herself.

As I watched Mother Josepha bustle about, nervously arranging papers on her desk, I quietly realized with a shock that what I wanted far more than for her to show us how to teach was for her to care about us, our loneliness and our worries.

You're dreaming, Mary, I scolded myself. *It's not going to be. This is the convent. People are not going to spend their time thinking about your feelings.*

I stared at a picture of an ancient nun hanging on the wall in back of Mother Josepha's desk and reminded myself that I wasn't the first poor soul forcing myself to listen to lessons I wasn't interested in hearing.

Just as Mother Josepha began her lecture, someone rapped imperiously on the classroom door and whispered a sibilant message to her. She grimaced, sighed and said, "Sister Mary, a priest is here to see you. Try not to be too long."

I managed not to grin, but I was thrilled. Two of my friends had already been visited by a parish priest who had known them before they entered the convent. Now, I also would be in that magic circle where someone who had known me before I took the big step of leaving home would talk to me and help me to adjust. I rushed into the parlor where Father Reilly was waiting to see me.

"Tell me how things are going for you," he began in his kindly fashion, settling back in the cushioned chair, reserved for visiting clergy.

"Well," I blurted out, "the praying is in Latin and it is too long."

He looked shocked, and pursed his lips just the way that Mother Josepha always did when I told her the truth about how I felt. I got a funny feeling in my stomach.

"Give me an idea of your daily schedule," he said, placing his Breviary on the table between us. He stroked it absentmindedly as if he was trying to send me a silent message of how much he liked praying, even if it was in Latin.

I tried to think of an acceptable reason that would explain my own lapse in fervor. "The bell rings at 5:30 in the morning, Father, and we have to rush to chapel for early prayers," I said, eager to go into even more detail about my difficult life to someone who I thought would be sympathetic.

He interrupted in a superior tone, "Don't you air your bed?"

I was stunned. *Why is he talking about airing my bed? What does that have to do with praying in Latin?* I felt embarrassed that in addition to everything else I was failing in, I was also remiss in housekeeping.

Aloud I said, meekly, "I don't have time to air my bed, Father. I'm cleaning, learning new Latin hymns and praying almost all day. My bed is in the attic. I have one tiny window that even Mother Josepha can't open. There are twenty of us up there rushing around using two bathrooms in the morning. There is hardly time to breathe, much less to air beds. And we are not allowed to return to our cells during the day to do any housekeeping chores that we omitted."

I had a lot more to say but I had run out of breath. Now he was looking embarrassed as if he had suddenly pictured a gaggle of young women, trying to hitch up their skirts lest they trip on their shoe laces, with their veils slipping off their wild hair. I wondered if we would return to the question of what I should do about my problem with praying in Latin. An unworthy part of me longed to remind Father Reilly that in the rectory he had a housekeeper who did all the lowly household chores for the priests, including airing their beds.

Maybe he would feel better about my adjustment to convent life if I told him that I was doing a lot of things right. Mother Josepha praised me only last week because my cubicle was so neat. Wasn't neatness a prayer in itself? That was the week I had stowed all my clean underwear, prayer books, old letters that I couldn't bear to part with and other pieces of what I knew Mother Josepha would call "junk" inside the folds of my comforter and put an old pillow on top of it all to hold it down. I heard my cell-mates snickering softly that day, while they listened to Mother Josepha congratulating me as I sat primly with my hands folded on my lap and hoped she wouldn't inadvertently reach over and topple my masterpiece. It was a system I invented to give myself more storage room than the narrow shelf of the closet that Claire and I shared.

Mostly though, I hoped that somehow I could make him feel better that he actually sponsored someone like me as a candidate for this convent. It was no use. He kept glancing at his watch and trying to suppress a yawn. He gathered up his Breviary, and slipped it into his overcoat pocket. I knelt by his chair and he made the Sign of the Cross over my bowed head as though that was the best he could do for someone so weak in her commitment to this convent life. I had no answers to my problem about praying, but at least I could tell my friends that Father Reilly hadn't told me that I should think seriously about returning to my home.

Father Reilly hurried out the old-fashioned parlor door to the outside world.

Men, I thought to myself, *are not likely to understand this life, especially if they are visiting with someone like me, who "mouthed off" even in the mild way that I just did. Could other sisters who are as mixed-up as I am help me to understand convent life? Maybe Jesus*, I concluded, *is the only one I can truly depend on; or is He? Sometimes He just seems like a silent figure I have loved and known who now wanders in and out of my life at will."*

Father Reilly never came back to see me. I would have to line up other people that I could depend on in this new life and find ways to talk with them, if I ever was going to make it as a nun.

I hurried back to the classroom where Mother Josepha already had begun instructing my classmates in the intricacies of teaching religion to little wigglers in elementary school. Father Reilly's visit had distracted me, but I was determined to ask Mother Josepha one or two questions. I raised my hand to get her attention.

"Mother," I said, "How do we get the youngsters in the class to listen to us?" She got a funny look on her face and, pursed her lips the way she always did when she didn't like something I had asked her or, worse yet, derailed her line of thought.

"Sister," she said holding up her clunky rosary beads and sighing loudly. "Have your lessons well prepared every day and the children will surprise you with their attention."

I hope so, I thought to myself. *But I'm not so sure.* Somehow her answer left me more insecure than ever.

If only my practical sister were here to tell me not to take Mother Josepha's sighs so seriously.

"Just find someone else to answer all your questions," my sister would have told me. But my sister was not in the convent, and I was. So Mother Josepha was my only hope.

As usual, she continued to ignore questions that she didn't feel comfortable answering. Still, something inside of me began bubbling in excitement at the thought of having my own classroom and some responsibility at last. Nervous and insecure as I was, the notion of teaching still filled me with the wild fervor of a beginner who thinks that after the first few weeks, everything will be easy. Enthusiasm had gotten me into the convent in the first place. Would it help me when I was in a classroom all by myself with fifty kids? I didn't think Mother Josepha and her rosary would help me then.

As soon as her overview of the diocesan curriculum in religion was finished, Mother Josepha passed out dog-eared copies of the Baltimore Catechism to each of us as sample textbooks. As I glanced at the opening pages, I recognized the same rote answers I had proudly rattled off when I was in the first grade.

Ah, I thought with relief. *It is all still true. And I will be teaching these truths to others.*

There had been rumblings in the Church recently, requesting a more liberal interpretation of these very doctrines. I had wondered, when I was told that I would be teaching religion next year, if I would be faced with embarrassing questions about changes in Church teachings. I felt unprepared to be challenged about religion. I had such trouble understanding convent regulations and making them fall into a pattern of reality. I didn't want to worry about changes in the Church, my bedrock of stability.

Mother Josepha spent several minutes of the last period of the morning assigning us to new seats for the rest of the week. Claire, who was quite tall, was shunted to the last row of our packed classroom, far from me. Betty and I were directed to separate sections near the door. We wanted to sit close enough to one another to trade comments, but Mother Josepha was too wily to make that kind of mistake. She thought even the smallest deprivation was "good for us." Anything to make our life difficult was valuable; she called it "teachable moments" and prided herself on using them. Poor Ann was plopped right in front of the teacher's desk, a placement that should have been a valuable lesson in how to separate friends in our future classrooms.

I have so little time to talk with my friends about my worries that I almost forget what they are by the time I'm legally allowed to chat, I grumbled to myself. *I'm supposed to talk with God during silence time which is most of the day. The only time when I can pour out my concerns to my friends ends up being a scant half-hour. And I can't even sit next to the person to whom I want to be chatting. How can I live my life like this?* I muttered to myself in a moment of semi-despair.

I wanted to talk to Claire and Betty about teaching religion, in a world where everything outside was slowly being turned upside down. I kept on carelessly turning the pages of the little catechism while I waited for the seat arrangements to be completed. Finally, Mother Josepha rang her bell to signify that our morning lessons were concluded.

At last! I said to myself. Somehow I did not think that I would be a great success at teaching religion.

It was time for us to proceed silently to the chapel and examine our consciences, admitting to ourselves any betrayal of our dedication to the rules and asking forgiveness for our failures. We knelt quietly at our prayer benches where I began examining my conscience. Thoughts of my little brother, whom I rarely saw now, kept popping into my head. Mother Josepha always told us that if we longed to see someone, it was a sign from God that we should say a prayer for the person.

But I didn't want to pray some soulless prayer for my brother. I wanted to actually see him, run after him in a game of hide-and-seek, and listen to his shrieks of laughter when I caught him. I wanted to sit in the last row of our old parish church and listen to him ring the bell for people to come up to the altar railing for Holy Communion.

"Tell me if I'm ringing the bells loud enough," he pleaded, and I told him later what a great job he did. I wanted desperately to have the lovely privilege of watching him grow up.

Mother Josepha's thinking didn't make sense to me. Maybe I would "catch on" to her philosophy someday and become a really good nun. Was that what I was supposed to do? A few tears slid down my cheeks. It was too late to examine my conscience. I followed my companions into the refectory for another wretched meal and wondered if I could ever learn how to be a real nun.

ANOTHER DAY, ANOTHER SUBJECT

The next day, Mother Josepha scheduled us for lessons in art and music, as well as for a continuation of instruction in teaching religion. Sister Seraphina, Mother Josepha's sister, taught both art and music and was eager to instruct our group. We secretly had been warned by two of the novices, who had been here a year longer than we had, that there was a price to pay if we challenged Seraphina's authority. Sarcasm was one of her weapons and she used it when we least expected it. She had a lot of power. We could be "put in our place" with penances from Mother Josepha if we were reported as disrespectful to Sister Seraphina.

Despite unpleasant rumors about Sister Seraphina, we looked forward to anything that would break the terrible monotony of constantly trying to be good. Examining our consciences twice a day only increased our sense of failure. The faults that we picked out of our tortured souls were stupid things like taking a sip of water when it was not scheduled, or raising our eyes when someone near us dropped her prayer book. Nothing we did ever was right. We were off-balance all the time, caught somewhere between being children and stretching toward adulthood. When endless prayers failed to help us handle our upside-down world, we resorted to humor. It was our salvation and our comfort when accompanied by stealthy smirks and shared giggles from friends.

Our friend Ann had an Irish sense of humor and found a sly way to make us feel as if we were in the driver's seat, even when Seraphina treated us to a bit of sarcasm.

"Look," Ann said one day, pointing out with a grin that the pictures of the Virgin Mary that Sister Seraphina drew looked suspiciously like the art teacher herself. "She has the same nose, the same sneaky, too-sweet smile, the same slightly off-center eyes."

Our other friends decided that Sister Seraphina probably had been looking in the mirror when she drew those pictures. It became a game with us to sneak around the convent to see where the art teacher had posted more and more new versions of her pictures of the Virgin Mary Seraphina for our edification. We giggled every time we saw one of them. It was our mild way of getting even with her for her unkindness.

When Sister Seraphina was not busy drawing pictures that looked eerily similar to her, she devoted herself to teaching us the diocesan curriculum in art. We made elaborate art books under her guidance to illustrate the various types of artistry she wanted us to demonstrate.

One day, she gave us an assignment that touched upon our imaginations. "Draw a picture that you remember from a story-book," she directed. After a moment, I recalled a scene from Hansel and Gretel where the artist had drawn several branches of a spindly tree emerging from each end of the picture, with Hansel and Gretel in the center of the drawing. I drew my own version of the artist's picture, portraying lost children in a forest of swaying trees menacingly bending on either side of the innocent children.

Sister Seraphina screamed in laughter. "These are only two half-trees," she chortled. She held my drawing up for a few minutes. No one else laughed. I wanted to cry. *Doesn't she see Hansel and Gretel? I* asked myself.

But I'm good at art. Why is she making fun of me?

I was too naïve to understand what was really happening. Where were all the saints whose examples always helped me before I entered the convent?

If I complained to Mother Josepha, she would tell me that God was trying to teach me humility, and bombard me with her favorite quotations from saints who would prove her right. Besides, it was her sister who was berating me, so could I expect Mother Josepha to be fair? Was this the life that I bargained for on the day I got in the car with my parents and came to the novitiate with Claire?

Maybe it really was. Maybe being hurt once in a while was part of the whole package. When I asked Ann, "Do you think Sister Seraphina knows that we make fun of her?" Ann simply shrugged.

Then she blurted out, "Don't you know, Mary, that Mother Josepha would have us sitting on the floor eating every meal if she found out that we laughed at her sister?" So I struggled on, in my teen-age way, to deal with Seraphina's classes that had so swiftly turned into something that would hurt me.

What should I do when we have music courses with Seraphina? I asked myself as we filed into the crowded organ room. *I know music theory already. Maybe I shouldn't raise my hand. I don't want to get into trouble, and most of all I don't want to be embarrassed.*

I decided not to let Sister Seraphina realize that I already knew the concepts that she was so grandly presenting to the rest of our class, as if she were a female personification of Mozart. I was beginning to learn how to "play the game," in order to handle some of the threats that arrived cloaked in Seraphina's ego.

Maybe if I hide my talents, things will go more smoothly for me, I told myself. But somehow, I thought, no matter what I did, Sister Seraphina would do something to me, that I didn't like. And I was right.

My dream of learning how to play the organ was placed in front of me like a delicious dessert and then snatched away as soon as I made the mistake of acting happy over private organ lessons.

Sister Seraphina gazed at me with narrowed eyes and calmly told me, "You can practice for one hour but only when I tell you it's okay. Today is your first practice period." She pulled her woolen shawl around her bony shoulders and walked out.

She left behind a rough diagram of the function of the various knobs and pedals. It was my only lesson that day, but suddenly I didn't care. I crumpled the diagram, stuck it in my prayer book and never looked at it again.

I was so proud. There was no one else in the chapel, just me. I pulled out all the stops, booming the hymns as loudly as I wanted. It was great fun, with no one to stop me and correct me. I made believe that I was playing in a grand concert with a glorious soprano, her bosom heaving as she tried to keep up with my trills and arpeggios on the organ keyboard. I paged wildly through the hymn book, looking for my favorite melodies, and singing them loudly, along with the imagined soprano. I was like the mad organist in the old ghost stories.

It was the first time in months that I had been able to do something without a superior controlling me. No one ever complained about the rowdy noise coming from the organ loft. Seraphina herself gave me only one other practice period. No more organ lessons were offered to me. I was labeled as "ORGANIST" on my official transcript and felt woefully inadequate for months because I didn't know how to use the foot pedals properly. But my moment of freedom on the massive Motherhouse organ lightened my heart and gave me a glimmer of hope that things would change for me, somehow, someday. All I needed was a window of opportunity to keep me happy, with its joyous promise of things to come.

The year wore on. Some of the lessons were in literature, introducing us to children's stories, ancient myths, and fairy tales. In the beginning, I was delighted by renewing my acquaintance with those astonishing parts of my childhood, when I again heard all those stories that my mother had read to me. Mother Josepha quickly let me know, as I wiggled in my hard wooden seat, that she was not happy with my knowledge of the literature being presented. She was annoyed with me for knowing every story she read.

Am I making her nervous? I asked myself, and began to sit quietly.

She rushed on and on hurrying through the exciting stories of magic animals and fearsome dragons that my mother used to read to my sister and me on rainy afternoons. When my mother read us a poem about the North Wind, she made her voice tremble with impending dread, and we began shrieking with delicious fright after the first few lines, yelling "Stop, stop." My mother gave us a love of good literature, with all its delights.

Mother Josepha hurried frantically through the curriculum, trying wildly to finish it before we were sent out to teach that following year. She pushed us to focus on the moral lessons that she was combining with those deathless stories and famous poems. She spoiled all the beauty that I so loved.

It doesn't have to be, Mary, I told myself. *When you are finally teaching, you can read these stories to your own classes.*

I began to tamp down my enthusiasm while I was in Mother Josepha's classroom and simply listened. It was a discouraging time. I still loved hearing those old stories but I didn't participate in the classes. No one noticed, and Mother Josepha may have decided that at long last I was trying to be humble. Maybe I was instinctively practicing survival skills in a hostile environment. I didn't spend time analyzing the reason why I held back. I knew only that Mother Josepha was uncomfortable with me in the class so I gave up.

Our only other teacher that year was Mother Josepha's sister, Seraphina. I had talent in some of her areas of expertise and could have profited from her knowledge. She treated me with derision whenever possible. Anything to put me down. It wasn't hard to make me feel inferior. Like a good nun, I tried to remember the suffering of Jesus on the cross. I said some extra prayers. But, in the end, I thought of my mother and her honest praise of me. I remembered the piano lessons for which she and my father had scraped together the money to pay. I fantasized having a fine old piano in whatever convent I was assigned to in another year or so. Maybe it would even be tuned, which was a luxury my parents rarely could afford. I thought with delight of my mother's boundless happiness when she finally had a piano in the house. It was then that I felt comforted. And I moved on.

There was one class in which I needed constant help; that was the sewing class. I didn't understand what we were doing. We were told to make a book of stitches ending with a hemming sample that would help me to impact the beautiful white habit that I dreamed of receiving in another year. The sample was a miniature version of one gore of the skirt of our habit. In order for the skirt to last, we had to sew a hem on the bottom of the gore. This would keep the skirt itself from wearing out. Where was the rest of the skirt? The whole thing didn't make sense to me.

Betty, one of my friends, came to my rescue. Her experience in a large family helped her to understand everything that would save clothing from running its life span before its time had come for the rag bag. I had helped her to complete all the music theory homework and she returned the favor by showing me how to finish my sewing book. We were like two poor souls who discover, just as the trolley car conductor gruffly asks for our fare, that we each have an extra dime in the lining of our jackets that will save us from the indignity of ejection from the crowded car.

I entered the convent convinced, as only the young can be, that I already knew everything I needed to know. I quickly found out that no one valued my skills. All my talents in music, art, and literature garnered me no praise from Mother Josepha or from Sister Seraphina. Instead they were ignored. For some reason, skill at sewing and hemming were more important to them than all my talents put together. If I were able to sew, and keep my clothes in perfect order, the superiors could breathe a sigh of relief and say, "At last, she is on the pathway to simplicity." My friends dragged me along that pathway for my own good, and I handed in my sewing book pretending a competence which I owed to Betty's practicality and kindness. I used to be so honest. Now all I cared about was getting the job done. The music teacher thought that Betty understood the intricacies of music theory and congratulated her on her book that actually I had finished for her. Neither of us cared just as long as we weren't caught doing each other's homework. It was like being back again in high school where cheating was okay.

When my first year in the Motherhouse was over I was prepared to teach a whole array of elementary school subjects to a class of fifty or more students. I learned lessons in frustration and humility. I figured out how to placate superiors whose last nerve I had probably irritated daily. I accepted various penances in order to deserve entering into a second year in the Motherhouse, where I could learn additional lessons in obedience and aggravation. I prayed myself into submission when I was close to responding with rudeness after I had been corrected one too many times or was lonely, hungry, or tired, all of which were constant conditions with me. I managed to make a few more friends despite the dearth of talking time. I still wanted with all my heart and soul to be a nun. In my quiet moments, I dreamed of reading wonderful stories to my students and admiring their drawings and telling them if they worked hard on the other lessons I gave them I would bring a new book into class every week. I comforted myself.

LAUGHTER IS THE BEST REVENGE

A few months earlier, we were carefree teenagers. Now we were obeying rules and regulations that, in our hearts, some of us secretly considered stupid. Occasionally Ann said, "Some of this is gobbledy gook, Mary," and the Irish part of me guiltily agreed.

The classes with Sister Seraphina were the most difficult to bear. In that setting, humor bubbled up more and more often as our antidote to frustration. Laughing at the wrong time often was met by frowns or by monastic penances, but the chance to put things into perspective was worth it. The most hilarious incident occurred in Sister Seraphina's class shortly before we were to receive our white habits in a dramatic ceremony.

Sister Seraphina entered our classroom with a broad smile, looking pleased with herself.

"I have written a new song for you to sing at your investing ritual at the end of the month," she announced, her hand over her heart, looking annoyingly dramatic as usual. She motioned majestically to Betty to pass out mimeographed sheets and settled herself in front of the little organ at the front of the room.

"Follow along," she ordered in her high-pitched voice. "This is a bridal song you will remember all your life." Her words sounded ridiculous even to those of us who enjoyed being reminded constantly that we were soon to be Spouses of Christ. But it was the tune itself that startled us out of our daydreams of achieving early canonization. I had heard that melody at every Gene Autry movie for several years.

I poked Claire. "That's the tune to Red River Valley," I whispered.

Claire, who was usually so proper, suddenly burst into a flood of uncontrollable laughter. "Red River Valley," she choked out, and began strumming an invisible guitar.

A blessed lack of self-control swept over both of us and spread to nearly every novitiate in the solemn music room. Some of our friends began to slap their thighs and twirl their song sheets over their heads as though they were lassos.

A tall, skinny girl in our class stood up and loudly yelled "Yippee-i-o-i-ay."

The sister next to her yelped, "Ride em, cowboy."

The room, usually a sanctuary of silence, was wonderfully noisy. We felt ourselves burst with laughter; we rejoiced in our outrageous rowdiness. We made fun of Seraphina as a unit. For once, no one felt guilty. It was a lovely change.

Suddenly, Seraphina left the room, and then Mother Josepha appeared in the doorway. Our hilarity ended when we saw her furious face. Silence descended on the classroom. Then came the declaration of our punishment.

"You each will perform a public penance this evening in the refectory, in front of the entire community," Mother Josepha declared. No one said a word. We left the classroom in a huddled group, not even whispering to one another.

That evening, when we answered the bell for dinner we found that, instead of sitting at a table, we would be plopped on the floor with our chairs taking the place of tables. Five timid souls, who had not made believe they were on horses at a rodeo, ran from one sister to another during the entire meal. They served all forty-five red-faced miscreants with plates of curled up fish that had been cooked too long, waiting for service. Weak-looking twigs of broccoli that no one liked anyway were dangling over each plate. Water had to be carried with special care, because big feet stretched out beyond the limits of the so-called tables (chairs). None of us dared act as if we saw anything funny in our penance.

The faces of several of the older sisters had quizzical expressions as if to say, "What in heaven's name could you all have done, to merit a group penance like this?"

We kept our eyes on our plates, our legs, our feet, on anything but Mother Josepha's face glaring at us or Sister Seraphina's eyes that were suspiciously red. In some strange and wonderful way, we had won the battle over her endless onslaughts of sarcasm. We would never again have to pretend that a melody she tried to foist upon us as her own creation was hers.

"It belonged to Gene Autry, you hypocrite," we silently declared to Seraphina, who was sadly chewing her broccoli. Humor saved us, even in the midst of our embarrassment. We finally had got even.

GOING FROM BLACK TO WHITE; HOPE REWARDED

Sometime in May, Mother Josepha was scheduled to post a list of the names of those in our class who would receive the beautiful white habit of our order in a solemn ceremony on August 4th. Claire and I were sure we would be rejected outright from that great event, because of all our misadventures during the past year. Our half-hearted acceptance of ancient religious rules, our giggles and whispering in the corners when we thought no one could catch us, and our occasional pouty reactions to Sister Seraphina's sarcasm in our art and music classes were all marks against us.

"Can Mother Josepha tell us to wear our black dresses and dingy veils for another year if we can't convince her that we can persevere in this life? Can we be sent home?" I asked Claire. She knew all about corporate decisions from working in a prominent company before she entered the convent.

"She's been observing us all this year," Claire said quietly. "She probably scribbles notes about everyone and will tell the higher-ups if she thinks we should pack our trunks. She doesn't like either one of us."

I didn't answer. Claire was so practical. Everything was black and white to her. She always said that Mother Josepha should have been the head of a large corporation. We liked making fun of her, but the thought of her having power to make major decisions in our lives was frightening. I still believed Jesus was calling me to this life, and if He wanted me to wear this black outfit for the rest of my life, I would do it. Having Mother Josepha decide my fate would be a bitter pill to swallow. Who was really in charge here? Was it Jesus? Was it higher superiors poring over summaries of Mother Josepha's private notebooks and deciding that a few of us should be sent home, even though we still wanted to stay in this special life?

"It might be kinder, in the end to give them the news now," Mother Josepha might already be proclaiming in her pseudo humble tones to the Council that was responsible for making momentous decisions related to the acceptance of new members into the community. We waited nervously for signs that a final determination had been made about our worthiness to remain in the convent.

Another month slipped by and suddenly a notice was posted on the bulletin board outside the chapel. Claire and I elbowed our way to the front of the line, forgetting the etiquette rules we had learned long ago when our mothers were in charge of our manners.

"Our names are there, Claire. They are there!" I whispered hoarsely.

Everyone around us was talking about beautiful white flowing outfits, called habits, being made for us. We were so excited we could hardly speak.

"When can we tell our parents?" we asked each other. "Dare we ask Mother Josepha if we are finally accepted? Are we really included, after all our transgressions? Are the new habits only for the good among us, who never raised their eyes as they walked through the hallways or whispered in corners as we did?"

One by one we were called to the sewing room and Schotze, the old German sister who was in charge of the laundry, measured us for those white habits. She was crippled from a long-ago fall from an apple tree in the convent orchard, but she still had a welcoming smile for each of us as she tucked up the heavy mohair material and pinned it in place. We weren't allowed to talk to her, but we smiled until our mouths felt stiff the way they used to when we were at a parish event and were trying to entice some boy to come over and ask us to dance. We now had our partner for life. Our eyes were shining with excitement.

We left the sewing room and forced ourselves not to run shrieking through the halls.

"We passed the test," we told each other, "whatever that test was! We will get our new clothes on the same glorious day. Mother Josepha didn't reject either of us."

Claire and I exulted that we would be together for another year. Maybe now we would begin to behave more like nuns.

And then the second rumor burst out. We would wear wedding gowns, whatever style we wanted, but they had to be white. My sister made my wedding dress and my parents brought it to the Motherhouse so I could try it on. It was quite simple, like a plain dress you would find in the back of an old closet that someone had forgotten to clean out when the Salvation Army came to collect clothes for the poor.

But then I caught a glimpse of myself in the tall mirror that my father had brought from home and lashed onto the top of an old station wagon that he had borrowed from one of his friends so I could see myself as though I were in a bridal shop. I looked almost regal. No ruffles, no sash, not even a fancy rosette for the neck line. But it was me and my sister knew it. I think my mother did too, even though her hands were clasped in tight fists as though she wanted to tear that gown off me and take me home where I would be safe from this strange marriage. In a few weeks I would march down the chapel aisle, still wondering if I was doing the right thing.

I had trouble falling asleep the night before we received our habits. I knelt on my lumpy mattress and leaned on the splintery window sill. I peeked out the grimy little window and gazed at the beautiful courtyard Mother Josepha never allowed us to enter, with its delicate trees and flower beds. I thought about how blissful Betty had looked when she ran past me, her face all aglow, carrying the extra set of new clothes that Schotze had provided for each of us.

Am I that happy? I asked myself when I saw her.

I finally fell asleep thinking of momentous decisions and small worries. I had memorized the rules that Mother Josepha had drilled into us all week. They were mimeographed and bound in a neat little book, "How to Behave on Investing Day." Only Mother Josepha would have thought of making a book of rules to remind us of her orders. Now all I had to do was follow them on the day itself.

A DAY BEYOND BEAUTIFUL

The first rule for our great day was to not look at our parents as we sidled past them, dressed in our distinctive wedding gowns. As a special privilege, they could take our pictures, but we couldn't pose or smile or even hesitate for a moment to let our parents get an individual shot. The wind blew our filmy silk veils and showed off the curls we had carefully arranged that wonderful morning. We dared not look at our parents or smile or wave to our little brothers or aunts or uncles. We belonged to God that day. We kept our eyes open just enough that we would not trip and fall. The local newspapers took pictures of us, marching along with our thoughts focused on heaven. I kept yellowy, fragile pictures of that amazing procession tucked away for years.

Ann walked behind me. She had made us laugh at the pictures Sister Seraphina drew of herself, labeled "The Virgin Mary," that she proudly posted outside the chapel door. Ann's humor helped us not to be hurt on the days when Seraphina's sarcasm was used relentlessly against us. Claire was next; Claire the dependable one, who could be relied on to be realistic if we were taking Mother Josepha's scolding too seriously. Finally came Betty, who was from a large Irish family that had already been touched sadly by the illness of a child. She was there for us when disasters from our own homes clobbered us and prayer was not enough. We did not need a Mother Superior to tell us we were about to become Sisters. We already were.

We marched on, into the stone chapel with its wooden choir stalls and vaulted ceiling. Our parents watched us with teary eyes, as if we were leaving them forever. Slowly, they took their places in the special pews reserved for them. We walked past them and stood in formation down the center aisle with the familiar choir stalls on either side of us. Those stalls were where we had prayed and dozed off or made mistakes in our chanting and met the reprimands of Sister Seraphina the next afternoon in music class. This day was different.

The Bishop looked at us in our wedding dresses, proudly wearing our flowery crowns, and said in his loudest voice, "Do you renounce all the pleasures of life?"

We, who thought we knew what we were renouncing but really didn't know at all, chorused, in voices almost as loud as his, "We do." We plucked the crowns of flowers off our heads and in one grand motion, hurled them over our shoulders.

There was a little commotion in the row in back of us, where one of the Puerto Rican sisters stood. In a frenzy of religious fervor, she had taken her crown of flowers and torn it into pieces, stamping on the fragments over and over, crushing them into the convent carpet. We were a little scared. It was such a wild display of inner devotion. We hadn't known that kind of gesture could exist and were jealous that we had not done it ourselves. What a grand finale that would have been. We could have talked about it for years.

"Remember when we ripped up our crowns of flowers and proved how much we loved God?" we could have said. But it was too late for a histrionic display that was not part of our culture. We would have looked ridiculous. She looked wonderful. Holier than we would ever be.

Mother Josepha motioned to us, and we followed her to the huge stack of white habits that was just to the right of the Bishop. He placed them on our outstretched arms and we carried them carefully back down the aisle, past our parents and through a small side door that opened into a large room. Older sisters each of us had personally chosen waited there to help us slip out of our wedding gowns and into our beautiful white habits.

We did not bother to catch the precious wedding dresses as they slipped to the floor. They would be scooped up by others later and put aside for next year's ceremony in case someone lacked a gown.

Suddenly I wanted to snatch my own dress with its precise little stitches and keep it forever.

I will look at it when I miss my sister, I said to myself. But it had already been taken, and put in the crumpled pile of dresses on a nearby table.

The helping sisters placed spotless white veils on our heads. We were speechless as we looked around the room and saw both ourselves and our friends transformed into nuns. It was an amazing moment that we could not describe to anyone who had not felt herself changed in a matter of a few seconds into an entirely different person. I gave one last smile to the sister who had helped me and walked with my class into the chapel.

The Bishop asked, as he held out a crown of thorns to each of us, "Sisters, will you accept this crown of thorns?" and we shouted our jubilant answer, "Yes, we will!"

Mother Josepha and several other sisters placed the crowns of thorns firmly on our white veils while the choir sang triumphantly the ancient monastic hymn, "Te Deum." We prostrated ourselves, face down, on the chapel floor and prayed for our families, our friends, the world, and ourselves. When we arose, breathless with joy, we processed triumphantly out of the chapel into a huge room that was set up with chairs and small tables.

Our parents and friends waited there to greet us and embrace us in our hard-won beautiful new clothes. We felt awkward, searching for words to describe our swirling feelings, emotions that we could not pin down. The time with our parents began to feel too long. We needed to run off and be with others who understood what had just happened to us, the wonder and excitement of it all. We escaped into hostess duties to calm our nerves. We jumped up, bringing our parents bologna sandwiches on white Wonder bread, along with tepid cups of coffee or tea. They acted grateful, wanting to be kind to us, afraid we might be embarrassed at the convent's stingy offerings on such a glorious day. Our parents' silence protected us from being hurt, as though we were still children. When the visiting hours were over, the chapel bell interrupted the last dregs of conversation. Our parents hugged and kissed us. We did not realize how much we missed such loving embraces until that moment.

Even after this long afternoon, we still were expected to return to chapel for more prayers. We were so excited that for once in our convent lives, we did not complain, even to each other. This would be the only time that all fifty of us would be chanting together with a group of fifty more sisters who were scheduled to make their vows in another few weeks. One hundred white-robed sisters, singing an ancient hymn to the Blessed Mother would march in a dramatic procession down the broad convent aisle. Our eyes would be half-closed, our hands hidden in the soft sleeves of our new habits. And we would be part of it all, part of this magnificent pageant.

It's like being in a movie, I said to myself. For once, I was not day-dreaming. This was real life.

That evening brought the final event required by monastic custom in our religious community, the shaving of our heads to symbolize our becoming "Brides of Christ." We had each chosen a friend who would perform this task for us in the privacy of our cubicles. Mother Josepha thought we would be unspeakably nervous at this point, silent in our narrow cells. Instead, the whole evening turned into a free-for-all of wild running up and down the corridors. We popped out of our curtained alcoves, amid shouts of laughter, our hair carelessly chopped off. Strands that had escaped the scissors of our untrained barbers were trimmed carefully to complete the job. Clippers appeared to finish the task and leave our heads devoid at last of any hair. The friends who did these honorable tasks for us arranged opaque veils over our shaven heads, and fastened them with a few snaps at the napes of our necks.

Ann ran up to me, yelling, "My haircut is finished! Do you want to see?" Before I could gasp out a startled, "No" she whipped off her filmy head-covering. But the haircut wasn't finished; it hadn't even been started! There she stood, her curly locks still intact, grinning in her inimitable way. We hugged each other and pranced down the hallway, calling out wildly to our friends. Mother Josepha finally gave up trying to calm us. The holy demeanor that she thought we would have at the end of this most pious of days had dissolved into poking fun at each other as we wandered around like happy little plucked chickens, our shorn heads covered carelessly by short veils. We knew that our hair would grow back, our new veils would fit more comfortably, and no one could ever tell us to shave our heads again. The day ended in a haze of joy.

A Whole New World — Or Was It?

After I received my beautiful new clothes in an emotional ceremony that convinced me I was destined to become a nun, I waited for the upset feelings and confusion that had bothered me for months to disappear. Instead the certainty I felt when Mother Josepha placed my new clothes onto my outstretched arms in front of the whole congregation slowly faded.

"Where have those happy feelings gone?" I asked myself. *"Am I always going to be dissatisfied?"*

I felt disgusted with myself. I was turning into an eternal whiner. I began going over the parts of my life that I had hoped would change when I received my new clothes. But Mother Josepha was just as annoying as ever and would be in charge of me for at least another year. All the old rules remained in effect. The only thing changed was that I had moved into the next level of monastic life, the level that would lead to my taking my first vows. I needed to talk to Claire and Betty and Ann. I was still so mixed-up.

The monthly Visiting Days with my family were never long enough. We all wanted more time with one another, and there was none. Certainly not for my shy, mild-mannered father who tried to squeeze in a few emotional sentiments amidst the chattering of the rest of the family. An unexpected glimpse of my mother sobbing into her handkerchief one month, when the bell tolled the end of visiting, disturbed me for days. How could I comfort her? I was taking more and more steps into a life she didn't understand. This was not a teen-age love affair like the ones that Claire and I bragged about to all our girlfriends when we lived at home. This one linked us with Jesus.

I sent a silent plea to my mother, "Please understand."

I waited day after day for the mix of mild depression and excited joy to settle down into a manageable mess that I could handle more easily. Finally, I simply accepted being in an up-and-down emotional state, taking as my daily mantra one of my Irish grandmother's wry sayings, "Hope for the best and expect the worst." Somehow it fit my sentiments exactly. A little caustic, but real.

In an effort to raise my spirits, I tried focusing on the bright spots of my official entrance day into the community. One of those moments was the bestowal of a new name on each of us. Like my friends, a few weeks earlier I had given three names to Mother Josepha. From those three, she chose my new name. I waited anxiously to hear the one she selected for me announced from the altar. The bishop boomed out my new name in his stentorian tones, "Henceforth, you will be known as Sister Edward." "Edward" had not been my first choice, but my father was all smiles when he heard his name bestowed on me. I hadn't realized how much it would mean to him.

I'm glad Mother Josepha picked it, I admitted to myself. *It isn't every day that she does something that I like.* To my surprise, a small wave of happiness washed over me when I heard it every day.

Some of us began to give one another nicknames that we used when Mother Josepha wasn't near us. It reminded me of being a teenager at home; there was a comforting feeling to it. I became Edwardo; it was my convent nickname.

"Hey, Edwardo," Claire would say when she wanted me to tell her the latest gossip. It was fun, like being a kid again. Claire never had a nickname, but she didn't care. She just liked being part of the mix, calling me Edwardo, and teasing me now and then. When I was able to snatch a few minutes with my friends, I bubbled with teen-age joy. I felt whole again.

Insecurity sneaked back when I heard Mother Josepha praising Sister Inez, one of our fellow novices.

"Listen carefully, as Sister Inez tells her story," Mother Josepha would say, and we rolled our eyes if we dared chance such a gesture without being noticed. Inez blushed and told us how she escaped from her secluded home in Puerto Rico because her parents refused to let her become a nun.

"I ran through a field once and plunged into an icy creek," Inez proudly proclaimed. "But I kept on running, trying to reach the convent."

"Didn't she know how to avoid thin ice?" I whispered sarcastically to Ann. "After all she was a country girl, wasn't she?"

Ann grinned and muttered, "Wait until she tells the part about her shoes."

And, right on cue, Inez described how her shoes were sopping wet by the time she got to the convent and took them off and greeted the Superior in her bare feet. I think she loved the whole thing, escaping from her parents, messing up the convent entrance with her wet feet, heroically defying her parents for Jesus' sake. It all sounded too exciting to be true. A few muffled giggles intruded at this point in Inez's narrative, which usually warranted frowns from Mother Josepha.

In the end, Inez's parents were notified of the whereabouts of their runaway offspring. They signed the required papers that allowed her entrance into the convent and brought a pair of dry shoes for their rebellious daughter, along with a thick envelope that contained Inez's dowry and supplemented the convent's expenses for finding her parents. The parents may not have enjoyed searching for her hither and yon, but the story probably delighted them in some dramatic part of their souls.

How brave our Inez was, how holy, and how we suffered, seeing her leave, I pictured her parents saying to relatives who gathered around to comfort them. Did they tire of hearing the details once again after a while? Secretly I was jealous, both of her great story, and of its reception by Mother Josepha. Or maybe I was just bored.

Mother Josepha, and even some of the other novices, continued to ask to hear Inez's story, but Claire and I couldn't match its drama. Besides, it made us feel inferior.

Claire used to whisper to me sometimes, after we had to endure hearing it yet another time, "She isn't any better than we are, Mary.*"*

But I always wondered. Sometimes, when we were chanting our evening prayers, I glanced in her direction and wondered if she was still thinking of her mother, sobbing alone in her lonely home faraway on a distant island.

I tried so hard to be good, like Mother Josepha kept telling us we should be. I hoped I would become kinder, gentler. Instead, when I received my new clothes, I was horrified when, instead of being filled with virtue, I was flooded with vanity. No matter how hard I tried, I was more a teen-ager than a nun. When I slipped on my beautiful white habit every day, I longed for a mirror so I could admire the way I looked for a few vainglorious moments. I had worn a dingy black dress and a threadbare black veil for a year. Now I had clothing I could hardly believe I was allowed to wear every day. At last, I was a member of an ancient order of religious nuns.

The fact that we had two official monastic outfits created a problem for me. One outfit was brand new, made just for us in Schotze's sewing room; the other one was old, with discrete patches where material had worn thin. "I don't think we have to wear the patched outfit when we see our parents, do you?" I asked Ann hesitantly one day, knowing the answer full well. I just wanted someone to back me in my exuberant plotting.

"I think we can switch them around," she said. "Especially if Mother Josepha doesn't know," she added with a sly grin. The next day was Visiting Sunday, when we would see our parents, so we decided to try our new system that day, wearing our best habits for our visitors and saving the patched ones for every day. It was a bold move, but we thought we could get away with it.

After Mass, the two of us rushed to our cramped cells under the attic eaves, frantically tore off our patched habits and exchanged them for our brand-new outfits. A few mothers who noticed the improvement in our clothing smiled at us in delighted surprise. Some of the other novices who were obediently wearing their patched clothing looked at us with puzzled expressions, but said nothing. They knew if Mother Josepha knew what we were doing we would be in trouble, as usual.

It was inevitable that our quick-change system would soon be discovered. When the next Visiting Sunday came, Mother Josepha burst into our attic cells, just as we were whisking off our patched habits in exchange for our nearly brand-new apparel to show off at our family gathering.

She screamed angrily, "What! You wear your patches for the Lord at Mass, and flaunt your new clothes to your families for vanity's sake?"

There was no proper answer to her tirade, and we knew it. We had known all along that we wanted to brag a bit. We blushed. It was a little like our high school days when we rolled up the waistbands of our uniform skirts so we would be more in fashion.

It was too late for us to change our clothes again that day, so we put on woeful faces until Mother Josepha disappeared, clattering angrily down the stairs. Then the two of us, dressed in our best habits, paraded joyfully into the convent parlor to see our parents. We grinned at each other all day. We had reverted into being the "smart alecks" of our teenage years.

You're still managing to be bold even while you're trying to be obedient, I thought. What a hilarious combination.

Our new clothes continued to absorb our thoughts daily, despite the sting of Mother Josepha's scolding. Even when we walked short distances, we practiced holding up our billowing skirts, lest we trip over them and tear their beautiful mohair material. We were so joyful. It made me think of the days when I practiced walking on high heels in my living room at home. I had felt so grown-up then. Now I was unsure where I stood in the lexicon of maturity. I knew only that at last I was in the clothing of a nun where I wanted to be forever. Maybe someday I would have a superior who would not judge my every action, unlike Mother Josepha.

As I slipped into my habit every morning, I wondered if my mood would be better that day. Once, in a moment of frustration, I wrote a sad little summary titled, "*Visiting Sunday as seen in the Eyes of a New Novice.*" I put it with my private papers. It was not a happy description.

Everyone arrives on the same day. My little brother is constantly shushed; my sister takes him for a walk; he breaks away from her and runs wildly up and down the convent halls. Friends spend only ten or fifteen minutes alone with me after a long train ride. My mother and father look at me with a longing in their eyes that breaks my heart. I ache to talk to everyone, but after Visiting Day I feel more isolated than ever. Nothing changes. Only I don't wear a black dress and a black veil; now, I wear a beautiful white habit. The loneliness has not changed.

Now that I looked like a real nun, I began to face what it all meant. Such control, such separation!

Mother Josepha, who rarely took the time to get to know us, had once sat at her end of the long table, chuckling loudly over little tidbits she read aloud from a letter Betty's mother had written to Betty, the intended recipient, who glared at the superior throughout the reading.

"Is she trying to be friends with us by sharing in our lives?" Betty muttered angrily under her breath.

In our more benign moments, we thought maybe Mother Josepha was lonely too, but we quickly returned to our feelings of fury toward her. We were too young to care about her needs. We were scrambling to meet our own.

Once, my mother said to me as soon as she saw me on Visiting Sunday, "Are you all right?"

I responded with my usual lie, "I'm fine."

She blushed a little as my father, in a patronizing way, commented, "I told you she was happy."

I longed to blurt out, "Mother, it's awful, but I'll get through it."

My mother sensed my turmoil but I couldn't be honest with her. It was another form of separation.

My sister who was tired of hearing me talk all the time about some saintly miracle worker, missed my quirky sense of humor and gave me a book on the famed Harold Houdini one Sunday, to distract me from all my pious reading. She thought it would be a good joke on how to escape from the convent; she didn't know that every book given to me had to be shown to the superior before I could read it. Mother Josepha wouldn't have caught on to the escape joke, but one look at Houdini's physique and I would have had to return the book with instructions not to let the family bring sexy books to the convent.

The more I learned about Houdini, the more I became obsessed by his prowess in breaking free, right in front of others. I imagined myself leaping up from my prayer bench and running out of that solemn chapel into the great outdoors where I could escape the endless hum of the chanting. Sometimes, when I was feeling desperate, I called myself Sister Houdini. The name alone gave me a feeling of blessed escape; but I was not Houdini. I wasn't even Edward, no matter what the convent called me. I was Mary, and always would be. No matter how hard I tried, I was far from being on the road to becoming a real nun, the nun that I had always dreamed I would be. Loneliness enveloped me like a shroud.

TRYING TO MAKE SENSE OF IT ALL

"Remember," Mother Josepha insisted. "When you were given your monastic garb, God gave you 'forever-and-ever' vocations."

I asked myself, one day, *What does this "forever-and-ever" thing mean?*

I thought I had until August before I took my first vows, and then two more years before I took final vows. That would give me a nice slice of time to think everything over before I made a commitment for the rest of my life. So why was Mother Josepha always talking about "forever-and-ever vocations," as though I were stuck in that box forever, from the very moment on Investing Day when we first received and put on the white habits? I almost felt as though I had been tricked into something. I needed to ask Claire or Ann or someone what it all meant. It was so mysterious. Didn't words mean anything anymore, or had I just been daydreaming when Mother Josepha had explained that strange phrase, "forever-and-ever vocation," one day? I probably had discarded it as meaningless, my usual system of dealing with religious formulas that I regarded as belonging to another century.

I began poring over some dilapidated books in our musty convent library.

Maybe there is an answer in one of these antiquated volumes, I decided hopefully. As I flipped through the yellowed pages, a sentence about temporary vocations that someone had underlined in red leapt out at me. "Forever-and-ever" vocations can be replaced by temporary vocations.

"What!" I exclaimed. "Why didn't Mother Josepha ever mention a temporary vocation to us? If that's the kind of vocation I have, I can walk out of here with my head held high. I can even leave tomorrow, if I want to." My heart pounded with excitement.

I began soothing myself with a few "temporary vocation daydreams." Maybe if I left the convent, some man would marry me and try to teach me how to be a good wife. I would have lots of children and never make them say long prayers. I would read to them and giggle with them over silly nursery rhymes, like my own mother did. When they were all grown up, I would tell them how I had a temporary vocation and Jesus persuaded me to leave the convent, where I was meant to be for only a year or two, not a lifetime. If I got angry at my husband, I would swathe myself in the white habit and black veil that I had squirreled away in a secret part of my old trunk, just to scare him into good behavior when he came home from work. It was a fun daydream, where I was always the winner, which was just the way I wanted it.

Or perhaps I would decide never to marry; then I would not have to ask a man what to think, the way nuns had to do with priests in the confessional. I would live in a spacious apartment, and give glamorous parties for lonely ex-nuns who had no place to go on Saturday nights. When they had all gone home, I would stretch out on a luxurious bed with a fluffy quilt, sip a glass of wine, and talk on my private telephone with my old friends.

The more I thought about the temporary vocations, the more eager I was to tell all my pals that I didn't have the "forever and ever" vocation, that Mother Josepha had told us over and over again had been stamped on our souls when we received our beautiful white habits. I had just the temporary vocation like it said in the book. Who was I to argue with God? I would show Mother Josepha the book in the library and tell her my decision was based on a theory that was already accepted by the bishop. She'd tighten her lips the way she always did when she was angry with me, but she wouldn't dare argue with one of the traditional convent books. I would whisper to Betty and Claire and Ann that I was leaving and show them where I had hidden the book about temporary vocations. In the end, Mother Josepha would give me a phony smile. I would give her one just as phony. Then I would pack my black trunk, call my parents, and go home.

"I had only a temporary vocation, Mom," I would tell her. "Could you please tell Dad I'm sorry if I'm disappointing him?" I would prance off happily and celebrate with a little party once I reached the apartment where I had lived for so many years with my family.

But it all seemed too easy. Maybe this was the devil tempting me. I told myself, *You had better start listening to Mother Josepha's lectures, Mary, just to be sure that your vocation is only a temporary one.*

I squeezed in beside Ann and persuaded myself to listen more carefully to Mother Josepha's lessons.

"Everything is God's Will," Mother Josepha was insisting in her whiny voice as if she sensed that not all of us agreed with her. *"He is trying to teach you lessons,"* and she would glance sharply at me. Maybe she knew what I had been reading in that book.

Part of me was still trying to understand her baffling rules for becoming holy; another part of me wanted to live my own life, free as a chirpy little bird, flitting from one endeavor to another. If only I didn't have to think anymore. What a relief that would be. Maybe I should be doing my own thinking. That was an even scarier thought.

The example of the other novices confused me. I loved them. They wore the same white habit. They chanted the same rhythmic prayers. But did they feel the same way I did? Was Mother Josepha's way of living this difficult life the proper approach to it? I wondered.

Her sermonettes always ended with the unnerving statement, *"Good sisters never complain. It is the way I have lived my life and I have never regretted it."*

Once I whispered to Claire, *"Is not regretting it an order?"* Claire snickered. It was hard for me not to be sarcastic. I said a quick prayer to a benignant God who I hoped would help me to hold my tongue long enough to escape to my cell where I could laugh by myself, or cry if need be.

I began to think back to my days at home when I was leading my carefree life. I went to school, teased my brother, aggravated my older sister, and tried to be my father's favorite child. Maybe I should just go home and give up the whole thing. Claire felt the same way, but when it came to actually walking out that door, neither of us could do it. We were afraid it wasn't God's will for us to leave and, more than anything, we both wanted to do His bidding.

And so we stayed a few more days, days that stretched into months. The prayers tore at our hearts with their beauty and their demands. The meals reminded us over and over that we were not at home any longer. We ached for our vow day to come, when we could make our sacred promises before the Bishop and receive black veils in place of the white ones we had worn for a year.

"At last, at last," Claire and I told each other, "we will feel more secure, even happy. We will understand that our tortured wavering was simply a test of our vocations. All along, we have been where we were meant to be. Too much thinking has addled our brains. Our vocations were the 'forever-and-ever' kind, not the temporary vocations that we dreamed of when too many rules and regulations wore our spirits thin. The days of questioning will be over."

Our dreams began to turn to the future. There were needy children waiting to be taught in some God-forsaken school in Brooklyn. Maybe there would be good food in our new convent kitchen. There would be open pantries and huge jars of peanut butter available all day and suppers hot from the oven and real ice-cream, not the kind that cut our tongues with slivers of ice because it was made in an old ice-cube tray. And the fish would not be left over from the meal that had been cooked for the priests and that they had rejected because it looked "funny." In our untried hearts, we suddenly trusted that our new assignments would be as wonderful as we had dreamed that entering the convent would be. We were ready once again to start a new life. But some of us still cried every day, asking ourselves if we really should be here.

MOTHER JOSEPHA AND THE SECRETS OF THE LITTLE RED BOOK

O n the last day in May, Mother Josepha announced importantly that she had a surprise for us. "Be on time," she demanded. "You are going to take another step toward becoming real nuns." My heart pounded wildly when I spied a little red book bearing the impressive title, *The Catechism of the Vows*, on each of our desks. I felt so important. Had we been judged worthy at last? Mother Josepha smiled at us as though we were becoming equals, and she hustled us into the room.

"You will be making your vows in August," she announced solemnly. "Chastity, obedience, and poverty," she stated, her voice suddenly trembling. She sounded nervous. Someone gave a little giggle that Mother Josepha ignored. After all, chastity had not been mentioned for a year and now Mother Josepha was going to have to explain how it fit into our lives. We were all interested in that forbidden subject and wondered with a certain measure of meanness, how Mother Josepha would stumble through that explanation. I groaned quietly when she cannily left its discussion dangling until obedience and poverty had been dealt with to her satisfaction.

Obedience had already been relegated to following convent rules for the most minor tasks, even when you thought you already knew all about such chores. "It is the humility that is the point," Mother Josepha had insisted to Betty one day, when Betty, the oldest of eight children, dared to say that she had folded countless hankies for her mother and didn't need lessons in that so-called skill.

"We will begin with the vow of obedience," Mother Josepha stated, holding up a handkerchief and showing us the proper way of folding it. "This may seem like a trivial example," she continued, "but it will give you in a nutshell the true meaning of obedience." Betty was blushing.

"This is pay-back time," I thought. "How mean!"

She scanned the classroom, momentarily pausing to gaze at Betty. "And, Sisters, God will continue to teach you through every Superior for the rest of your lives, even if it only involves the proper way of folding a handkerchief." She continued using examples from our lives to teach us how to follow the pathway to perfect obedience.

Folding a handkerchief in the prescribed convent manner I could manage, but being assigned to live in Puerto Rico was something I had not included in my lexicon of obedience requirements. One of my favorite high school teachers, Sister Callista, had been shipped off to teach physics in the Catholic University in Puerto Rico, with a side order to instruct little kids all about Jesus every weekend. She developed some kind of a curable lung disorder while she was there and was brought home for treatment in a New York hospital.

After she recovered and returned to Puerto Rico, she received a second phone call with the same ghostly voice saying "I need you, Sister Callista."

Her response, "Yes, Mother," was probably the one we were told to make if we received a similar phone call. My beloved Sister Callista never did learn Spanish and coughed ominously, but she still spent obligatory weekends with noisy youngsters repeating her fractured little phrases about Jesus. I never heard what happened to her.

Mother Josepha proudly began that week by having us practice saying, "Yes, Mother," to a make-believe call from the Motherhouse. One-by-one, we knelt by her desk with lumps in our throats, while she tested our resolve. She would smile benignly after we agreed cheerily to have someone else decide if we would live far away on a little island, for an undetermined length of time.

I wouldn't mind so much, I said to myself, *if I could live somewhere accessible by car or subway. It's the distances involved that make my stomach ache. And the big, ugly bugs, too*, I added if I felt honest.

Sometimes, people told me. being in the army was the same as living in the convent.

But it's not the same at all, I protested silently.

My sister used to tell me, after she gave birth to her first child, "You can read all the books you want, but until you push that baby out of your body, you are a sea of ignorance about childbirth."

When I was practicing Mother Josepha's silly method on how to accept an assignment to Puerto Rico, I remembered my sister's off-hand comments. Playacting was not reality, either in childbirth or in accepting orders to go to Puerto Rico. If only I had the nerve to make some flip comment to Mother Josepha while I went through the motions of agreeing to move to Puerto Rico, I might have relaxed a little. I needed to face the fact that, like the teacher from my old high school, I too might get that ghostly phone call from some nameless person in the Motherhouse.

The second vow that was carefully imbedded in our youthful psyches was that of poverty. Everything was jointly owned by everyone. Stalin would be proud of us. Even our books that someone dear had given us did not belong to us. They were only "for our use."

Mother Josepha had a special exercise to involve ourselves in on the last day of our instructions on the vow of poverty. We silently trudged to the trunk room to count our possessions. Surrounded by rows of dusty trunks that had not been touched for months, we assumed cramped positions, kneeling on the floor or sitting on rickety stools that we had dragged from various corners where discarded furniture was piled. On the floor near each of us were a few sheets of yellow paper upon which we could catalog our belongings.

Somehow, I felt virtuous as I counted my worn-out underpants, my stockings full of knobby darns, my fragile handkerchiefs that would not survive another good sneeze. After all, I was following the dictates of that strange vow of poverty. The fact that no sane person would want any of these pathetic objects of clothing did not disturb me. But suppose Mother Josepha told me to give up some of my precious books, or the little statue that my brother gave me when I left home. Then this whole bow to the vow of poverty would take on another meaning.

Under the innocuous term, "Vow of Poverty," the long arm of the Motherhouse could intrude on my joyous possession of a few trinkets that I had amassed in the past two years. A strange superior could distribute all my goods, meager though they might be. Mother Josepha never even glanced at my list, but that dreadful power was still hers. If someone could take my belongings, they were not really mine. I suddenly saw that vow for what it was, namely a kind of communism without the red flag and the Siberian gulags. All in the name of my benign Jesus!

I wondered. Was this what this Jesus that I loved really wanted from us? I would make the vow but I had a feeling that I would be re-interpreting it for the rest of my life.

It will take years until I lose my guilt over owning things, I told myself in a moment of shocked recognition of what that vow really meant. I didn't like the implications one bit, but I made the vow anyhow, hoping no one would expect me to keep it.

We closed our little red book at the end of June, after Mother Josepha made a few red-faced explanations of the vow of chastity.

We'll be taking that vow with about as much understanding of chastity as we had when we were in seventh grade morality class, I thought to myself. Old Sister Gertrude was forever blushing and the boys in the class were always hooting. No one was hooting now. A slight embarrassment settled over us. We barely knew our own bodies. I knew I wasn't getting married, so why give a class in calculus to students who needed to learn only the multiplication tables

What confused me were Mother Josepha's endless tirades about particular friendships. My friendships would be particular. Was I supposed to enjoy friendships only with people I barely knew? Then they wouldn't be particular. Finally, a ragged catechism that I found in the library one week rescued me from my ignorance. I grabbed Claire as she came out of the chapel one day.

"Claire, Josepha is talking about lesbians when she harps on particular friendships." The two of us blushed beet-red.

"So that's what it's all about," Claire gasped. "Glad we finally found out."

We linked arms and laughed and kissed each other innocently, the way we always did. We never told anyone else about our great discovery. Our vow of chastity was safe forever. As for Mother Josepha's worries, we could have allayed her anxieties, but it was more fun to watch her squirm when the word "particular" popped up in our classes on the vow of chastity.

The other half of Mother Josepha's harangues on chastity involved loving everyone equally, a goal that we decided belonged in a fairy-tale somewhere. When we accepted the walking companions that were assigned to us, she said. "God puts you next to the sister to whom He wants you to talk." In my early days in the convent, I actually believed that, until I realized how stupid it was.

Claire and I finally decided that love, the mixed-up everyday kind that we saw in our families, was the foundation of our vow of chastity. The antiquated rules that we struggled so hard to follow when we were novices began to fade away bit by bit. We hugged as many of the pathways to God as we could, including the ones in the little red book, proudly labeled, *The Catechism of the Vows*, and the ones that had slowly developed in our hearts as we were growing up at home. We loved one another and tried to be kind to those who were annoying us. We began to relax. Maybe things would work out. I hoped so. I could not live with this chaos in my soul.

THE GREAT DAY APPROACHES AND OUR NEW LIFE BEGINS

A month after we gently closed our little red *Catechism of the Vows* for the last time, the superiors invited our parents and friends to come to our magnificent chapel to witness our promises that we would be obedient, poor, and chaste for the rest of our lives.

I whispered to Claire when we could snatch a minute alone. "Suppose I kick over the kneeler in the chapel. God, I will be so embarrassed."

"If you do that," she whispered back, "I will kick my kneeler to keep you company."

That was the kind of friend that Claire was. Like we used to say when we were in high school, "One for all—all for one." We need not have worried. We practiced for hours every day until we could slide into our prayer benches with a precision that was equivalent to dancing on the head of a pin blindfolded. Our hearts were joyful. We wanted desperately to make this day perfect for our parents, for ourselves, and for God, Who probably was the One in that little triumvirate who cared even more about our happiness than anyone else.

The actual taking of the vows was preceded by ten days of rigid silence which Claire and I struggled desperately to maintain. Once or twice, when we were afraid we would burst if we kept our fears to ourselves any longer, we scribbled notes to each other and slipped them onto each other's prayer benches. It was chancy even to find a corner where I could talk to Claire, but I could tell by her pinched face that she was as scared as I was. I had believed for the longest time that this was the life I wanted to lead. The more the rotund retreat priest blathered on in his unctuous way about how safe and happy I would feel once I had made my vows, the more I questioned myself if the happiness he was talking about was the kind I wanted. And what was I supposed to be safe from? If I could go home for a few months and try out having boyfriends again, maybe I could settle down and know whether or not this strict life with the strange rules was really for me.

Claire and I listened to the retreat master drone on three times a day about the great burden of the vows and how happy it would make us to be bound by them forever.

"Will they really make us happy?" I questioned Claire in one clandestine note.

Claire scribbled back, "You're happy now, aren't you? And you'll be even happier then!"

I could feel the exasperation in her response. Maybe I was shaking the fragile foundations of her own approach to taking her vows. So I subsided and relied on my own inner feeling of peace that popped up whenever I really thought about this vow-thing. I had wanted it for such a long time!

I asked myself every night, *Will my life really be different after I make my vows?* I made mental lists of what to expect. The rules would still be the same, but maybe the food might be better. I'd be assigned to a new place to live, somewhere in the wilds of Brooklyn or even Queens. I wouldn't have a cent to call my own, but maybe my parents might live a little closer. I could even bump into them on the street. We would grin and say hello and then I would scurry on to the convent, which in my daydreams would be located on the very next block. Best of all, I would finally be teaching, which was part of my dream, since it involved some intellectual activity for which I had been hungering.

Dusting and polishing the convent banisters had never done it for me. The miserable lack of true humor in our superiors bothered me. I missed a good belly-laugh, and could barely remember any of the silly little jokes that had been so much a part of my life when I was in high school.

Most of all, I asked myself, *What will I ever do if Claire isn't sent out with me? She has been my pal*, I reminded God, *since we were girlfriends in high school and my stalwart companion all during the aggravations and frustrations of the past two years. I've been more conscious of her presence than of Yours*, I reminded Him one day in a burst of hopeless anger. But there was no answer. There was only the maddening response that Mother Josepha always gave us when we were nervy enough to say that we were disappointed because God had not answered our prayers.

"When God says no, it is still an answer," she intoned and pursed her lips and opened her own prayer book, ruffling the pages as though she hoped that some wise saying would spring out and help her give us a lesson in how to think.

Like the heroine of an old-fashioned soap opera, I buried myself in unlikely daydreams when I should have been praying frantically for greater peace. In those daydreams, Claire was always assigned to the same convent I was. I knew that was more than I could hope for. But fantasies were the way I dealt with difficulties. Fantasies and thinking that all the problems I encountered meant that somehow I would become holy and more worthy of belonging to Jesus in this mystical marriage that Mother Josepha was always holding up before us. Vague memories of my mother's determination during rough spots in her sometimes rocky marriage began to strengthen me in my own rough spot.

I can do this, I said to myself, *even if Claire is not with me.*

A welcome distraction erupted five nights before the vows ceremony. There was quite a hub-bub in the chapel near the confessionals.

"What's happening?" I whispered to the sister nearest me. She rolled her eyes expressively.

"Grace can't take her vows with us," she hissed. If only I could slide closer to Claire and get more information from a kindly source.

Gossip had always been a failing of mine, but only when the person being tattled about was not a friend.

Grace was a friend of ours from high school, intelligent, but not inclined to take convent rules too seriously. This time she had stepped over the line disastrously and read a book condemned by the Vatican. The only solution was to have a special priest come from the Bishop's offices in Brooklyn and give her absolution immediately.

We were salaciously curious. If only we could have a peek at that book. Was it like the latest issues of *Secrets in the Boudoir* that we hid in our school lockers when no one but us had the magic combination? We turned down the pages of that magazine for easy referral if needed.

One or two of the words we understood, and we gladly shared them with our closest friends. I remembered underlining the word, "nipple" three times to be sure my friends didn't miss the best parts that followed the *Trail of the Nipples* story. We thought we were so worldly, as we rejoiced in our wickedness. Our innocence was staggering.

But the book that Grace had been reading was largely in French according to my spies. We would never know why it was condemned. Maybe we could find an English version and giggle at the little priest hidden away in the Vatican who buried his head in his hands and persuaded himself to read the entire story out of fairness to the author before his book was ripped from the shelves of the Vatican library. Our superiors hadn't allowed themselves to even look at the title page lest they, too, become contaminated.

A solemn-faced priest arrived that night from the Bishop's office and Grace was duly absolved from her sin. The whole episode was behind her. It had been an exciting event for us in an anxiety–ridden ten days. She made her vows along with the rest of us. Unlike us, she knew the meaning of the Vow of Chastity and made her promises anyway.

BRIDES OF CHRIST AT LAST!

The next day, a group of us who had been friends since high school helped one another to arrange our white veils for the last time. We were like brides, in our flowing habits and our fluttering veils, as we waited to march down the long chapel aisle and be part of an amazing ceremony. Had it been televised we would have been both proud and humble to be part of it. Crowns of flowers were secured by a few pins on top of our veils.

We said in loud voices that echoed in that huge chapel, "We reject these flowers and ask for a crown of thorns..." Did we really mean it? Who knows? Does anyone really know what they are saying at moments like these? We threw our flowered crowns over our shoulders letting our stunned audience know that we didn't want those pleasures. We wanted only the thorns. No naughty pleasures for us! Mother Josepha obligingly hurried forward to place crowns of thorns on our veiled heads to replace the flowers that had been scattered on the carpet. I wanted to snatch just one flower the same way I kept the faded corsage from my senior prom. I would have kept it forever!

We were so joyful at the chance to show our parents how sincere we were. Our poor parents had struggled most of their lives to give us a good life. Now they realized that we didn't want that kind of life anymore. When we tried to explain to our parents that we were marrying Jesus, they looked at us with quiet disbelief.

One of the Irish mothers simply said, "It's not a marriage, dear," and left it at that. We brushed aside what she said, and devoted ourselves to our conviction that we were marrying Jesus.

There were many things that our parents had understood about us when we were home. They knew about our crushes on various boyfriends and our moods when the latest "love of our lives" stopped calling us. These were all things they understood from their own life experiences. But this marriage to Jesus was beyond their ken. We had woven a fantasy around the Jesus thing. We thought we understood it when Mother Mistress drummed it into us over and over again, but there was a little part of us that didn't believe it any more than our parents did.

Claire used to say quietly, "It's just gobbledegook," when she was frustrated by some of the stupid statements that were waved before us. "It's all a mixed-up message meant to keep us in line, Mary," Claire would mutter.

My first reaction was usually shock, but each time, after I settled down, I realized she was right. We became like gardeners and pruned away the beliefs that we somehow thought didn't belong in our lives. Marriage to Jesus was not one that we were willing to eliminate from our roster of firmly held convictions. Even "Claire the practical" kept that one alive in her fervent heart for many years, as did I.

We declared our vows in loud voices. We wanted our parents to hear us making these holy promises. We prostrated ourselves on the chapel floor, our faces pressed onto the rough carpet while the choir sang *Te Deum* to mark the glory of this submission of ourselves to God. It was a beautiful moment and not one that we ever forgot.

We marched giddily out of the chapel, trying not to run with joy. We belonged to Jesus at last. No one could take that away from us. I thought of the little holy card I had given to my parents on the day that I entered the convent. Its message, "I'm the Bride of Christ," said it all.

I spotted my parents and pointed to the hand-lettered sign in the hallway just outside the chapel that announced light refreshments for parents and friends. Someone had set up small circles of tables and chairs. A buffet table had been stocked with piles of sandwiches, bologna on Wonder bread, just like the day we had received our habits. Coffee pots were perking cheerily, and Styrofoam cups were carefully stacked along with plastic spoons and sugar packets. Someone had donated boxes of cookies. I managed to feel pride at the humble offerings. It was clearly a gala day. My parents were allowed to stay for an hour to visit with me. Was it finally obvious to them that I was happy in this strange life? They smiled stiffly, trying hard to share my joy because they loved me. My body was swathed in my white robes, my face almost hidden by my flowing black veil, my crown of thorns already askew. But their acceptance kept us a loving family forever. I hugged my parents and quietly said, "Thank you for letting me enter the convent." My father grabbed my hand and squeezed it tightly. I never remembered him being so demonstrative. My sister devoted herself to keeping my little brother from running into groups of nuns, as though he were a football player. And I, as always, was torn between the love I had for my family, and the amazement that overwhelmed me from having declared less than an hour ago " Yes, I am the bride of Christ."

A New Assignment, but Where am I Being Sent, and for How Long?

The mystery of where I would be assigned once I had made my first vows was kept secret until the last possible moment.

Where am I going to be sent? I frantically asked myself. I didn't have a clue where I would live, what grade I would teach, or if I would be with Claire, or Ann, or anyone else that I had privately begged God to send with me.

"Only if it is Your will, of course," I quickly added at the end of my petition, lest He get angry at me for being too pushy. I was always trying to placate Him, as if He were a combination of a benevolent father and a grumpy old codger.

Mother Josepha rushed into the room where all fifty of us were gathered, waiting in breathless anticipation to hear where we would live during the coming year. She began reading the assignments in the clipped tones that forewarned us not to ask any questions. She had read only five or six names when our gathering began leaking emotion, ranging from little squeals of joy to quiet moans of distress. Some sisters were being sent with friends; others were going to convents where they didn't know another soul.

Two Irish sisters were being sent to a forbidding fortress of a convent where, for the past twenty years, only Italian sisters had been sent. This had been Mother Josepha's inventive method of protecting Italian sisters from prejudice. I pictured her proclaiming to the General Council as they decided how to break the deadlock the Italian cohort had over the "Little Sicily" convent for years, "We should send one or two Irish sisters there, every few years, to balance all the Angelina's with a few Brigids."

I poked Claire and muttered, "I hope they know how to twirl spaghetti on a fork!"

She grinned. She knew that pizza was the only Italian food I could eat neatly without protecting myself with layers of napkins.

Mother Josepha blandly went on giving the assignments. Ann was being sent to a convent in a rough area of Brooklyn. She would be near the docks where sailors searched for quick companions and children learned curse words they shared with one another but not with their parents. That was an assignment I would have liked. It would have been full of adventure. I could tell exciting stories to all my friends while they wilted away in boring educational environments. The next assignment was Claire's. She would teach in a more subdued atmosphere that lacked the thrills that she had always laughed about when she told us stories of her work-life in the corporate world.

And I, I was paired with Betty who could whip up a meal, clean a room in a flash, and repair any rips in her clothing, and anyone else's for that matter. She had grown up in a practical home, where she was the oldest of eight children, and knew how to do many things that were foreign to me. I had always felt inferior to her. She had prowess in all the areas I lacked. We were so different.

Unlike Betty, I had not gathered practical skills in the years before I entered the convent. My mother, instead of getting herself a housekeeper, bought an eight-volume set of *Bookhouses,* which introduced youngsters to the great literary works, proceeding from nursery rhymes to Greek myths. My father bought sheet-music from popular Broadway shows and listened critically as I tried to tap out the tunes. On Saturdays, I didn't clean the exacting way that most other mothers required. Instead I dusted and vacuumed, with the radio at its highest volume blasting the latest tunes, while I danced around the living room pretending that I was a famous stage star. My mother decided early in my life that it was easier to do all the shopping herself, and abandoned teaching me how to cook. Instead she regaled my sister and me with stories from her treasured *Bookhouses.* If she felt devilish, she read us a few scraps of wonderful poetry that scared us into shrieks of delighted fear. I had not been prepared, as Betty had, for the practicalities of life in the convent. And yet Betty and I were paired. *Paired by God*, I told myself. How would this odd couple fare, leaning on each other in a strange new environment?

Mother Josepha rang her little bell and told us to pack our trunks for our new homes. I joined several other sisters, all of us in a state of high excitement, bumping into one another in the trunk cellar. We were eager to pack our meager belongings, ready to send them off to our new homes somewhere in faraway corners of Brooklyn, Manhattan, and Queens. Each of us had received a neat address label from Mother Josepha, with our name and destination on it. I felt a thrill when I saw the words, *Holy Angels Convent*, printed in thick black letters on the innocent-looking label. I dusted off the top of my trunk with an old rag someone had left on the trunk next to mine. Suddenly the trunk belonged to me again, like it had when it had been lodged in the corner of the dining room in my old home in Queens.

You and I are on the way to another adventure, I said quietly to the trunk. It had been filled with the dreams of a young girl two years ago. The trunk was unchanged, filled with old-fashioned clothes that had never worn out. But I, I wondered somehow, if I still belonged here. I closed the lid and fastened the brass clasps. It was time to move on to my next adventure.

A New Convent, But Not a Wonderful New World

Two older sisters hovered around the exit to the trunk room, eager to find out where everyone was assigned.

"Where are you going to be living?" one of them asked me excitedly.

"Holy Angels Convent," I answered proudly.

Their faces fell. They blushed.

"Is there anything wrong with that convent?" I asked, not sure if I wanted to hear the answer.

"No. It's just that no one has been sent there in several years." They both smiled. They looked as if they were sorry they had said anything to me. I was sorry too. I was nervous enough without their innuendos.

I brushed past them and ran until I reached the narrow stairs that led to our attic cells. I hoped I could calm myself before it was time to leave. It would be hard to see my friends after we left the novitiate. Once we lived scattered in convents throughout Brooklyn and Queens, it would be next to impossible to arrange visits. The sisters controlled contacts between convents, as well as letters and telephone calls. We had lived together for the past two years, and now our assignments to new convents made it like starting all over again; we had to try to find new ways to talk to one another. The loneliness of convent life began again.

Betty had remarked to me last week, "You're bored with this life, aren't you?"

I immediately felt judged. I wanted to shriek, "You feel bored too, Betty, don't you? For two years, we've been polishing banisters, practicing Latin hymns for the funerals of nuns whom we have never met, and enduring criticism by teachers if we showed any expertise in areas they were presenting. Of course I'm bored, and I'm angry, too." But I didn't want to lose this friendship by arguing over which of us was right with our reaction to the lack of stimulation in our lives. I dropped the subject and went on polishing the banister.

Whenever I told Mother Josepha I had doubts about continuing in the convent life, she told me it was just a temptation.

"Say some extra prayers," she ordered with an impatient sigh. "You think too much."

Her bland comment reminded me of the reaction of an elderly priest when the mother of one of my friends died, leaving seven sons and daughters under the care of their somewhat elderly father. When my friend turned to the priest for guidance, he said, "God wants you to stay in the convent." The fact that she was only 19 years old did not change his mind. Even I, still in the first throes of following the dictates of the superiors in order to achieve true holiness, thought his advice rather unrealistic. She did stay until she was forty years old, when she finally left the convent and married a former priest. Those were the days when thinking for yourself was never an option.

I thought fleetingly, *Whatever happened to the country custom where the bereaved father took a walk and came home with a new wife for his now motherless children?* It seemed an easier solution than having a teenage girl take over the duties of mother and housekeeper for many lonely years, and abandon her own plans for her life. When I asked my usual unwelcome questions about decisions that the clergy made concerning the futures of confused nuns, my thoughts, if they were even considered, were discarded as superfluous to the situations.

The elderly priests Mother Josepha brought to the convent to "straighten us out" as she called it, had a mechanical approach. They endlessly churned out automatic defenses of the convent manifesto, upholding their end of the bargain, as if their lives depended upon it.

One of the priests recommended that we read the Book of Job, a suggestion I had successfully avoided for the past two years. Maybe he thought that reading about Job and all his problems would make us realize that we should stop whining. Mother Josepha told us Job's story a few times when we complained about what she considered "minor trials." She was so condescending. Our little hurts and worries were summarily dismissed by her. But Job scared me. He was too accepting of the terrible trials that God sent him. In the end, he mysteriously recovered everything he had lost.

Perhaps Mother Josepha was right and I was mulling over all the rules and requirements too much. Martin Luther King's soaring rhetoric summed it all up in one simple sentence, "I have a dream." My own dreams about my future in the convent were rather mild, but they were mine, and just as precious to me.

I looked around my attic room to be sure I had not left anything behind. It was nearly time to leave. I said good-bye to the old window that I never could get open, and straightened the narrow mattress. It looked even lumpier now without its sheet and comforter. I put my final bits and pieces into a small satchel, ready for the trip to Holy Angel's Convent. My trunk had already been sent by the efficient Mother Josepha. A scared-looking postulant rapped on the attic door to tell me to hurry down to meet our "chauffeur," Sister Imelda.

"She's waiting by the cloister gate," she said nervously. I clattered down the stairs and ran out to the parking lot where Betty was already waiting for me, standing next to a smiling nun with her skirts pinned up to avoid the rusty car fender.

"Hi," she said. "I'm Imelda. "I'm your sister and your chauffeur."

She had just arrived in an old rattle-trap car to drive us to our new home in a down-trodden area of Brooklyn. All during that bouncy ride in a car that desperately needed new shocks and probably new tires as well, she gave us a spirited, lively account of life in our new convent. She had lived there for five years. Her comments about the grinding daily schedule, the unusual number of old sisters living there, plus a few other scary factoids, startled us, worried us, or made us grin, depending on the information she gave us.

As the three of us sped along the highway in the ancient convent car, Imelda mentioned in her matter-of-fact way, "When we get to the convent, we'll have a huge chocolate fudge cake and piles of fresh cookies right out of the local bakery. Eat a lot. Trust me. You won't get a chance to eat like this again for a very long time. Any treats we get are usually rock-hard left-overs from Subic's day-old bakery."

Betty and I glanced at one another. What could we say?

I thought wildly, *This is not something my mother did when we had company. She didn't go to a bakery where the owner pushed stale pastries on us that he knew no one else would buy. Is this our brave new world?*

Imelda continued chatting on. For some reason, I began to feel at ease. Imelda's stories didn't include all the platitudes that Mother Josepha added to whatever she told us so we wouldn't argue with her.

Imelda is one of the truth-tellers in our lives, I thought to myself.

Even more important she has a devilish sense of the ridiculous. For the past two years, I have been finding elements in convent life that I wanted to laugh at, when I wasn't too overwhelmed by guilt to allow myself a moment's levity. Maybe Imelda's honesty will help me to strike a balance. We might even laugh together at the awfulness of some of the rules, those rules that I tried so hard to believe in for two years.

I am going to find real sisters in this life, I said to myself. *Will Betty and Imelda be two of them? Whether I am in the convent or somewhere else*, I decided. *I will always have sisters.*

As the car sped through our new neighborhood, I grimaced at the sight of the old tenements with their dirty windows. Bits and pieces of laundry dangled from the handle-bars of bicycles that rested against the rusted railing of balconies. Imelda whizzed past them, trying to beat a red light. I settled back in the rigid car seat, glanced at Betty, and wondered if we would have a chance to talk later. I hoped so. Maybe our cells would be nearby and we could sneak in a few excited minutes of reactions before it was time to go to sleep in our new home.

Imelda continued to drive us through the dark streets of Brooklyn until we screeched to a stop by a nondescript –looking building.

"You're home," she said with a mysterious little chuckle that made me wonder what awaited us. We scrambled out of the car, dragging our suitcases behind us. Into the convent parlor we went, with its polished chairs and pious pictures on the drab walls, and through an adjoining room with an old-fashioned upright piano with which I would become all-too-well-acquainted as the months went by.

Finally, we reached the community room with its long wooden table and several straight-backed chairs placed carelessly here and there. Imelda led us to the head of the table where a grumpy–looking nun was sitting. She was wrapping several large cookies into a paper napkin and shoving them willy-nilly into the sleeve of her habit as if it was some kind of a secret pocket.

"This is Sister Waltruda, our superior," Imelda announced to us. She continued the introductions as if we were at a gala affair. She pointed to me, "This is Sister Mary," and then touched Betty gently on the shoulder and added with a smile, "Here is our other new member, Sister Betty."

She gave both of us a modest push towards Waltruda, who greeted us with a gruff hello, and asked loudly, "Can either of you play the piano?"

"I can play a little," I admitted, hoping I would be allowed to use the old piano I had seen as we hurried through a maze of rooms to meet her.

Waltruda smiled briefly at my answer like the inscrutable Cheshire cat in *Alice in Wonderland.*

Then she turned to Betty. "Do you like little children?" Betty who was the oldest of eight children answered with a joyful "Yes," but our brief interview was already over before either of us had a chance to say anything else.

Everything she wanted to find out about us was already discovered. Imelda grinned at us as if to say, "Never mind. This is the way Sister Waltruda greets anyone new. Don't feel bad."

Sister Waltruda pushed the cake-box, some plastic forks and a few paper plates nearer to us. Only a few slivers of chocolate cake were left, along with some broken cookies.

Couldn't the other sisters hang around long enough to find out our names? I asked myself sadly. I took the nearest fork and plate and began quickly claiming some of the frosting on what was left of the welcome cake, lest Waltruda eat that too.

Suddenly, another sister burst into the room and yelled, "Betty, I didn't know you were coming here."

I felt left out immediately, but the wave of loneliness vanished when Betty's friend, Sister Liguori, turned and hugged me as if she had known me for years. I was grateful to be included. Would the feelings of isolation that I had endured these past two years be swept away at last? Suddenly the frosting on the cake tasted more delicious.

I am happy just to be having a treat on the first day in our new home. Maybe everything will be all right, I thought.

Sister Waltruda stood up, muttered something about her arthritis and declared loudly that we had taken a long time reaching the convent. She was obviously blaming us for her tiredness.

You're not the only one in this room who's tired, I said to myself rebelliously.

I wasn't getting off to a good start, feeling resentful towards my superior so early in our acquaintance. I looked around the room. It didn't look at all like a gathering place where people waited excitedly for new members of the community to join them.

Only empty plates remained now, scattered on the community-room table. In the novitiate, we never had cake. Cookies and miniature bars of candy were given to us once a week in what I remembered as an embarrassing free-for-all. I remembered a few young sisters coming into the room on Sundays, carefully balancing trays of goodies precariously over their heads. As soon as they deposited the precious treats onto the long wooden tables, we rushed towards them with a wildness that our mothers would have been ashamed to see. Those with the longest arms snatched the most candy and the largest cookies and eagerly slipped them in their desks. We were like a bunch of barbarians, gathering at the gates of a town, ready to take our rightful share of the loot. It was a memory I was ashamed to recall.

But this rude greeting in Holy Angels Convent was worse. At least in the novitiate we were all kids, with our adolescent manners. Now I was in my new home, where I would live and work, pray and eat, smile and act like an adult.

"Hey, I'm the guest here," I longed to say, looking at the empty plates, the dreary remainders of our pathetic little feast. "How about me?"

But of course I said nothing. Sister Waltruda was as oblivious to her breach of etiquette as Mother Josepha had been to the rude grabbing in the novitiate for the biggest cookie or the most candy bars. "To the victor belong the spoils" had been the rule on Cookie Sunday; apparently something similar was the rule in my new home.

"Sister Imelda will show you your cells," Waltruda said gruffly, turning back for a moment as if she felt my irritation at her rudeness, and wanted to make things right. But I was wrong. She only wanted to make sure that she saw me in the morning so that she could give me my assignment for the coming year. I was uncertain if she was innocent of any meanness towards me. If I knew she cared, it would have made me feel softer towards her.

"I'll see you in the morning to give you your school assignments for the year," Sister Waltruda said and left the room, brushing the last few crumbs of that delicious cake from her ample bosom.

I thought of an ancient relative who used to keep a luscious cake high up on a china cabinet when we visited. She offered us only one skinny piece of cake when we visited her. I never liked her. She was too tight-fisted. Now I was comparing Sister Waltruda, whom I barely knew, to that long-forgotten woman. Had I always been so critical of people? Was the convent doing this to me, or had this always been me? I felt like running home until I could figure myself out. I calmed myself down and marched up the narrow stairs, led by Imelda.

What an odd beginning! Betty and I took turns blurting out questions.

"Is everyone else already in bed?" I asked. I felt a little hurt. I tried not to sound judgmental, one of the many faults that Mother Josepha was always trying to bully out of me. Try as I might to persuade myself how fine our greeting was, I knew there was something wrong with the so-called "welcome party." Maybe there was something wrong in my being in the convent, any convent. Maybe I didn't belong in this life at all.

Why did these sisters go to bed before Betty and I arrived? And why did God send me here to live with them? I thought. It usually comforted me to think that He managed my life, but today I felt like a ship without an anchor. *If I only I can hang onto Betty, Liguori and Imelda, maybe I can survive. And I will have Jesus, too,* I reminded myself, ashamed that He was the last one I remembered on my list of helpers.

Imelda continued to shepherd us along a narrow hallway waving her hand casually towards a row of four toilets that were fastened against the wall, their plywood doors swinging loosely. Each door was just high enough to shield the identity of the sister sitting on the "throne" behind it. The tops were open.

"Those are our bathrooms," Imelda said, and we paraded past them as if having toilets that were not enclosed in private cubicles was normal.

At least they aren't outhouses, I comforted myself. But I felt horrified, anyhow.

Mother Josepha would have scolded me fiercely if she knew my reactions to those unconventional bathrooms. Like an eternal conscience, she was always with me pursing her lips and shaking her head at what she called my "worldliness."

"Forget your high-and-mighty attitude about those sanitary arrangements," she would have said, "Be grateful these toilets are not in the backyard and you along with them, waiting in line, for all the neighbors to see."

I had a quick vision of rows of poorly clothed children, hopping from one foot to the other, waiting for a chance to hurry into the communal toilets, with me at the end of the line. I longed to find out Betty's reaction to the strange toilets, but decided to wait until the next day to ask her what she thought of that ridiculous arrangement. We followed Imelda quietly towards our rooms. We were tired of asking questions.

Like Topsy in *Uncle Tom's Cabin*, the convent building appeared to have "just growed," with no architect's plans to guide it. Nothing in our lives seemed to have any design to it. Our first meeting with Sister Waltruda, our first meal of scraps of crumbling cake after a long car ride, our first tour of the house itself, with its jumbled arrangement of rooms all whirled in my mind like a bad dream. I was too worn out to make sense of it all. I dragged myself to bed and hoped I could find the chapel in the morning. It was a creepy beginning.

AN INAUSPICIOUS FIRST MORNING

The bell the next morning jarred me out of a confused sleep. Somehow, I stumbled into the chapel and slid onto an unoccupied kneeler in the first row. Betty was next to me, dutifully turning pages in her book and whispering the Latin words of the psalm for that day. Sister Waltruda was in the back of the chapel, where she could spy on us and be sure no one was stealing a few extra minutes of rest. I tried to turn around to get a glimpse of some of the other sisters through sleep-blurred eyes, but it was too awkward. Maybe they would introduce themselves later in the day.

Sister Waltruda rang her little bell, and meditation began. I fell asleep, my head bobbing uncomfortably.

A bony finger poked me sharply in the back, and a harsh voice hissed, "Wake up." I could hear heavy shoes clumping back down the aisle as the owner of the finger returned to her seat. My first morning in my new home and someone had already decided to correct me.

I mumbled, "Thank you," like Mother Josepha had always told us to respond if someone pointed out an error in our behavior, but I wanted to scream, "Leave me alone."

Betty gave me a little poke in the arm to let me know she was on my side in this daily struggle with sleeping during prayers. She understood me.

Prayers and Mass dragged on. At last we went to breakfast. Sister Waltruda was too busy slurping down her cereal to pay any attention to us, other than a sharp glance at Betty when she dropped her cereal spoon on the hard linoleum floor.

Liguori gave us a big grin and mouthed the words, "See you later," as she squeezed past us on the way to deposit her cereal bowl in the refectory sink, and hurried out to marshal the older kids into her classroom. Two or three of the other sisters looked kindly at us, although they didn't know our names, yet.

It will be all right, I told myself. I was like someone who whistled as they passed the graveyard. I hoped that what I was afraid of existed only in my imagination.

I gulped down the soggy remains of my cereal and tried to pay attention to the reader for the day. She was droning in a nasal monotone about someone named Maximilian Kolbe, a Polish priest, who Imelda told me came from Sister Waltruda's hometown. Maybe Sister Waltruda had dug potatoes as a youngster in the same stark fields in Poland, as did her model of holiness, Maximilian Kolbe. I began picturing Waltruda in a raggedy apron, loading potatoes into a torn burlap bag, squinting at the sun. The reader went on mumbling about the humble Maximilian who worked in the fields all day and studied theology in his spare time in the evening, as he pored over thick volumes of religious works by the light of a sputtering candle. I liked only the potato parts of the stories. That was the Irish part. It was the only section with which I really connected. The rest belonged to Sister Waltruda's forebears, not mine. The reading dragged on and on until all the cereal dishes had been scraped clean. Betty and I had enough of the sainted Maximilian for one day.

"Are Polish saints the only ones we are ever going to hear about?" I whispered to Betty as we brought our dishes to the cluttered sink to wash them. Betty rolled her eyes and grimaced.

Finally, Sister Waltruda rang her little bell to signify that breakfast was over, and the day began.

"Sister Mary," she announced. "Come to my office this morning at ten o'clock for your September assignments." Imelda winked at me as she carried her cereal bowl to the cluttered sink. It was comforting to have a friend interested in how I felt about my assignment.

I HAVE MORE, AND MORE ARDUOUS, ASSIGNMENTS THAN MOST

As I waited outside Sister Waltruda's cramped office, I continued to wonder how much she would tell me about my predecessor, Sister Tess, the peculiar fourth grade teacher whose place I would take in a week.

"Sister Tess," as Imelda had referred to her the day before while we were bouncing along on the trip from the Motherhouse, "is on a rest cure."

I thought rest cures were carried out in insane asylums where all the inmates were huddled together in one barren room with a hard-backed chair for each of them, and a few stony-faced nurses watching them. My grandmother used to click her tongue when she and my mother read about them in the local country newspaper while we were on vacation in the summertime.

"Oh, dear," my mother used to say, "is Liz back in the asylum again?" and the two women sighed.

Now I listened carefully and willed Imelda to go into more detail. "Sister Tess enjoys a permanent vacation. She lives her own life in our convent, does whatever she pleases, reads, snoozes, takes little walks, while the rest of us slave away in what used to be called the Lord's Vineyard."

Wow, I thought. I felt shocked, but still hoped that Imelda was just embroidering the story. She continued with even more upsetting details.

"Two or three of Sister Tess's students run home every few weeks to escape the miasma of mental peculiarity that pervades Tess's classroom. The kids say Tess makes them nervous. She doesn't scream at them or hit them. In fact, she does her best not to have anything to do with them. They sit on their wooden benches and sneak glances at their wooden teacher, and run home when they can bear her strangeness no longer. All they know is, they have to leave and their parents don't know what to say."

Imelda didn't explain Tess's behavior any further; she stopped at her scary description of little kids running home to get away from a peculiar teacher. I felt shocked, but nothing more was added to the strange saga of Sister Tess and her run-away students. I didn't ask any more questions, just gulped a few times and thought about those children that night. I wondered if any of them would be "left back" to repeat the parts of Tess's lessons that they missed while they were running home.

Sister Waltruda knew kids left the classroom, but couldn't find a substitute for Tess. She waited until the September school term began, hoping that a new sister would be sent. When Betty and I appeared, as if by magic, Sister Waltruda promptly assigned me to the new fourth grade class for September. Everyone was happy. Tess was already safely settled in the convent, removed from an intolerable assignment for which she was probably unsuited by temperament and from which she had finally escaped. I was a new face in the school and relatively unknown to the parents. Sister Waltruda probably considered my arrival as an answer to prayer, if she had even worried about it at all, which I doubted.

I thought about Sister Waltruda, that strange woman, and knew she was a mystery I would never solve. But I was getting an inkling of why people looked alarmed when they heard that Betty and I were assigned to Holy Angels Convent. Even if they didn't know the story of the fourth grade teacher, they may have heard rumors. I wished I could pack my trunk and go home. There were some odd sisters here, and I was afraid that Sister Waltruda was the strangest one of all. She was the one who had all the power over me. That was the scariest part of all.

While I waited nervously outside Sister Waltruda's office to receive my official assignment for the year, my mind was awhirl. When the door finally opened, Sister Waltruda gestured to me to stand in front of her desk while she reached hurriedly into the loose sleeve of her habit, where she had shoved cookies last evening. She pulled out a crumpled handwritten list.

"You'll be teaching the fourth grade starting next Monday. Fifty-three students will be in your class. I'm hoping a lot more may sign up by the end of the month." She smiled her weird Cheshire Cat grin.

Why is she smiling? I thought. *I can't teach such a big class. Can I possibly wiggle my way out of this assignment?*

Suddenly, the training of Mother Josepha that had been thoroughly instilled in me these past two years popped out and I reminded myself, *I have to obey Sister Waltruda no matter what she orders me to do.*

The night before, when Betty had innocently told Sister Waltruda that she enjoyed little children, Sister Waltruda had responded with the satisfied smile of a victorious general after an easy victory. This very morning, Betty learned she was scheduled to teach 55 first graders in the mornings and another 40 wigglers in the afternoon. Also, I had sneaked a look at a list on Sister Waltruda's desk while I was waiting for her; it gave me the astounding news that Sister Ligouri was being assigned to teach 65 seventh and eighth graders crowded into one large classroom.

Suddenly, having to teach a class of 53 fourth graders, with even more to come as the days wore on, seemed less unfair to me. I said nothing, smiled weakly, and took the list of names of the fourth graders I would be teaching in a few days. I struggled to remember what Mother Josepha had drilled into us about our assignments being gifts from God, designed to make us holy. A nervous feeling stirred in my stomach. I had never quite believed in that story about God fixing our lives to make us holy. My Irish Grandmother didn't believe in that kind of religion. She had contracted typhoid fever when she was 22 years old and borne a retarded son as a result. All her beautiful red hair had fallen out. She never complained about wearing a cheap brown wig for the rest of her life, and she always had a funny quip or a kind remark for others. There was a bravery about her that I learned more from than from any of Mother Josepha's platitudes.

If only I had the gumption to whine a little. Whining always won the day when my brother was irritating my mother. It wore her down. But something warned me that Sister Waltruda would win every altercation. The only course of action that made sense to me was to obey this strange woman and hope the more normal sisters in the convent would help me muddle through my daily life here. Mother Josepha's favorite canards sounded so reasonable while we were in the novitiate, far from reality. Now her platitudes sounded unrealistic. I looked at the scribbled list of names again.

I can't even pronounce some of these names, I thought. *Will their parents have heavy accents? Will I understand what they are saying to me?*

Anxiety flooded through me, as I thought about the roster of pupils; parts of the list were underlined in red for some secret reason that would probably be explained to me when it was too late to beg for another assignment. I was beginning to lose hope already. I felt like crying out, "I can't do this impossible job!" But I could act like that only in my wildest fantasies. I was a nun and had to do what I was told to do.

I was about to ask for a blessing and leave Sister Waltruda's office when she gave me a triumphant smile. "You said last night to Sister Imelda that you can play the piano. Giving piano lessons every day after school is an important part of your assignment, Sister."

She handed me another crumpled piece of paper with scribbled names on it and dollar signs after each name.

"Here is your after-school schedule," she said, as if she was doing me a favor.

I'll be teaching wild little kids how to play the piano after I've taught other wild little kids to read and write all day, I said to myself angrily.

Imelda had told me the day before that the only time to talk with the other sisters on school days was the first fifteen minutes after school was dismissed in the afternoon. That was when I could gulp down a quick cup of tea, chew on one of Subic's tooth-cracking cookies, and chatter about our classroom experiences until the bell for silence rang again, cutting off conversation for the next four hours.

How did I get into a life like this? I thought in despair.

As if she could read my mind, Sister Waltruda added slyly, "And don't expect to have time to eat a cookie. You will need to prepare your music room. Not a minute can be wasted." I looked at her and wondered why she was so mean.

I won't even get a chance to talk to Betty. I will be in a panic, putting piano pieces on the music rack in a nervous rush and piling any extra loose music sheets anywhere that they will fit. My treasured metronome will teeter on top of the piano. I had been so proud of that metronome when my father gave it to me for my tenth birthday. I already worried that it would be damaged if it fell.

"I'm looking for more children to take lessons," Waltruda added blandly. I dearly wanted to say, "Won't the parents be angry if too many kids are crowded into the piano classes? It will mean that they don't have as much time in the classes with their teachers."

But I could tell when she glanced at me that she was concerned only with how much money she could make, not with the quality or quantity of teaching received by the children.

My mind wandered for a moment remembering what a piano meant to me when I was living at home. My parents had given me piano lessons on an old Knabe piano that my mother had bought for $10 from a neighbor who was moving the next day. That piano was the joy of my life. I took lessons happily from an inventive woman on the next block who rewarded her students with Hershey bars when they did well. Once I entered the convent, any chance of playing the piano vanished like a puff of smoke, until the fateful day that I saw the upright piano in the music room of my new home. In my naiveté, I had pictured myself playing some of my favorite tunes in my free time. It was not to be. There was no free time in my future, and the piano was not mine.

Like everything else in the convent, the piano was not there for my pleasure. Instead it gave Sister Waltruda a glorious opportunity to add to my daily duties, gleefully signing up any stray child for piano lessons. When had Simon Legree escaped from the story books of old and taken over Waltruda's mind? Apparently he was teaching her how to wrest the last ounce of energy from an already exhausted nun and make a little money at the same time. I hadn't even run a lemonade stand when I was a kid. I had no defenses to battle a slave driver like Waltruda. I knew only how to say "Yes" to her every command.

Suddenly I understood what Betty meant when she said yesterday that I was slated to be the convent money-maker. The precious minutes after school—when, theoretically, I could talk with other sisters—I actually prepared the parlor as the classroom where I taught little kids to play the piano. If I talked too long, would Waltruda glare at me and point angrily at the music room? Would there be time to arrange my precious metronome on top of the piano and fix the music sheets neatly on the piano rack?

If I relaxed at my piano bench for even a few seconds, would I fall asleep, my head drooped over the keyboard and my veil askew, just like I did in the chapel when I was supposed to be praying? There would be no Betty kneeling next to me, poking me, to save me from being embarrassed when a little urchin giggled and tried to wake me up. I would be as oblivious to the noise of that piano-banger happily pounding on the old yellowed piano keys as I was to the low murmuring of more alert sisters praying around me when I was in the chapel. What could Betty do to help me when I slept in the middle of a piano lesson?

Miserably exhausted and always hungry, I was firmly ordered to give piano lessons to wriggling boys or girls every afternoon, after I taught 54 youngsters in my crowded classroom all day. I was like a character from one of Dickens' stories with no one to complain to except Jesus, Who had gotten me into this whole mess to begin with. If only Imelda would poke her head in the door and wink at me, just to give me relief from this awful situation at the orders of this awful woman.

As Sister Waltruda turned to close the door to her office that morning, she paused and gave a finale worthy of her efforts to squeeze the last bit of energy out of every sister who still drew breath.

"You like singing, don't you?" I nodded in eager agreement as I fell into the trap. She pulled a sheaf of music out of her sleeve, and handed it to me.

"Good," she said. "The organist quit last week so I expect you to play the organ every Sunday, and of course teach the music for Sunday Mass." I almost burst out, "I can't do it, I'm so tired, and hungry.... Please don't give me anything else to do." But I took the book she was holding out to me and didn't say a word.

The term ALTO was emblazoned on the top of every page.

I've always been a soprano, I thought. *Now, in the magic world of Waltruda, I am suddenly transformed into an alto. I'll teach a motley group of sixth graders to warble the alto section of each hymn. Those two brief organ lessons that Seraphina grudgingly gave me in the novitiate will finally be put to use when I struggle to play the huge church organ with all its mighty pipes and old-fashioned stops. My God,* I mumbled to myself, *there is something wrong with this woman. There is only one thing I can do, and that is to accept my new role.*

I took the music-book from Sister Waltruda, and later managed to sing the new music out loud in my little room for hours. It was nearly dawn when I finally felt I could fool the "choir" into thinking that what I was forcing them to sing really did match the notes on their mimeographed music for Sunday's Mass. I wasn't sure if anyone in my group could read music, but I kept hoping they would be able to match a few notes to what they were singing.

My perfectionist tendencies were already beginning to wither like autumn leaves as Sister Waltruda multiplied my assignments, but for the first few days I told myself, *I will still try to be the perfect nun with a real choir.*

Deep inside, I knew the whole assignment was pathetic. The endless teaching, the piano lessons, singing fancy harmony with a group of rag-tag youngsters who probably could barely read music, Sister Waltruda's bizarre method of giving out assignments, the isolation—everything was far worse than at the novitiate where at least I could hope I wouldn't be noticed. What had I done to deserve this wretched place, this unbelievable assignment, this peculiar Superior who ignored the reactions of helpless sisters to miserable jobs? I was caught in a box like Houdini when he was trying to escape. But he broke loose. Unlike him, I could see no way out. I had just made my vows, and it was too soon to leave. And did I want to anyway? My heart was still caught by the mystery of dedication to an ideal. I was very far from abandoning that ideal.

*   *   *   *   *

As I left the room, Sister Waltruda called after me. "Sister, do you and Betty like to walk?" At last, a normal question!

Does she really want to know what we like to do? I said to myself, pleased at the thought that she was thinking of us.

But it was another trap. She said, with a glint in her eye, "You and Betty can walk to Normal school every Saturday, because New York State requires that anyone who has not yet mastered college courses in teaching learns the fundamentals of formally preparing young women be teachers. Or, if you want to, you'll have carfare but only one way. It will be your choice," she added magnanimously.

I felt my stomach lurch, like it used to when I was close to vomiting as a child. But I didn't want her to know how close I was to losing control of myself.

I dearly wanted to ask her sarcastically, "Is this at last the end of our interview now?" but all the brashness that occasionally popped out when I was at home, if I was arguing with my parents was gone. The docility that I had depended on when I was a dreamy teenager, planning how I would fit into the role of a nun, was gone too. I needed to talk to Imelda or Ligouri, who might have the answers that I needed. I almost believed Sister Waltruda was acting rationally, until Betty and I talked to Imelda later that day and discovered that the walk to Normal School was two miles, one way. Imelda looked disgusted when she realized how we had been tricked into thinking that Waltruda had been doing us a favor giving us a choice. Usually Imelda could be counted on to laugh, but this time she just squeezed our shoulders in a kind of sisterly hug, and said nothing.

There are times when there is nothing that can be said, I thought to myself, *and this is one of those times.*

In the end, as Betty and I trudged along every Saturday to Normal School, we quickly discovered to our astonishment that our long walk actually was a delight beyond description. We could walk together, gossip all the way, and ride home on the bus, still chattering, unencumbered by rules of silence. It was like a miracle. We could talk, and talk we did endlessly, breaking carelessly into each other's sentences, knowing we forgave one another with joyful giggles, at our new-found freedom.

The fact that we had already been up for more than an hour , rattling off morning prayers by ourselves, meditating for a few mandatory seconds, and eating a piece of Subic's stale bread for breakfast, was small payment for the luxury of gossiping as much as we wanted for hours. What a blessed relief from the unnatural silence we endured every day. And it had fallen into our laps simply because we humbly accepted an order from a thoughtless superior. Maybe there was a kindly God after all!

Sometimes, on the way to Normal school, we stopped at a beautiful Armenian church. We loved going to a bit of the Mass there and listening to the wonderful harmonic music. Once we reached Normal school, we shouted greetings to our friends who lived in different convents from both Brooklyn and Queens. One or two of the cooks in those convents sent thick tuna sandwiches for us, festooned with dripping mayonnaise. Big pickles wrapped in wax paper were slipped into the box to add to our glorious meal. Sometimes the sandwiches were roast beef from a special meal at that convent. And the cookies! They were plump and chewy with raisins or nuts. We could not believe such largesse existed in other convents. Sometimes we entertained everyone with tales of Waltruda's eccentricities and became the comedians of our group. No one had stories like ours. We were the queens of humor, feeding our friends with stories of real life, far from life in their staid convents. Our payment was the rapt attention they gave to our every word. And their love for us fed us even as we gobbled down the wonderful food they brought to us. We were fed, body and soul.

On the way home we discussed what their suppers, or even Sunday dinners would have been in those lucky convents. We fell upon our lunches greedily on Saturdays, talked and laughed, rejoiced in our friendships, learned more about teaching, and rode the bus home to within ten or twelve blocks of the convent. We stopped at Subic's day-old bakery with its dusty shelves and stooped old ladies waiting for their orders. Subic ambled out to the front of the store and handed us the greasy cardboard boxes of what he referred to as the "treats for his ladies at Holy Angels Convent."

"He thinks he just bought his ticket to Heaven," Betty joked as we walked with arms outstretched, trying to keep our clothing safe from chocolate smudges left by Subic's unwashed fingers.

We knew that we would be greeted with excited smiles when we came through the convent door with some sugary treats. It was a strange world, and we were part of it. We liked being the bearers of goodies for the others. Our Saturdays were such good days for us. They were our life-savers. Did anyone else have such happy days? We considered ourselves blessed.

When Sister Waltruda had finished giving me my assignments, and declared that Betty and I would be given carfare for only one way when we went to Normal School every Saturday, I didn't argue. I didn't complain about the piano lessons, or the choir teaching, or the threat of bigger and bigger classes. I was no longer afraid that I would be sent back to my parents. I was finally adjusting, feeling "at home" in this strange existence that I had so longed for when I was a teen-ager. I accepted what I had bargained for when I made my vows and tossed aside the pleasures of life along with that fake crown of flowers that each of us had bravely thrown over our shoulders at our investing when our parents and friends so admired us. Reality, with all its bruising components, was settling in.

WHAT CAN WE EAT AND WHO SHOULD WE EMULATE?

I *wish there was more time to talk to one another*, I thought to myself one day. *There is always something either Betty or I want to share.* As we left the chapel one day, she whispered to me that she had asked permission from Sister Waltruda to accept two shriveled apples that one of the first graders had given her as a gift.

"Guess what Sister Waltruda said when I asked her for permission to keep the apples," Betty continued.

Waltruda muttered, "You had three apples on your desk this morning, Sister. What happened to the third apple?"

"She questioned me as though I were a noted criminal. She must have been counting those dried-up apples when she passed my desk." Betty blushed as she continued her story. "I told her I was hungry and had already eaten one of the apples. Then I knelt to ask her for a penance because, before I even had permission to keep the apple, I had eaten it. Guess what! She told me I could have the apple and give it to a friend." And, with a smile, Betty handed me the apple.

The story upset me, but I ate the apple anyway. I was too hungry to turn it down.

Suddenly I felt outraged at convent rules that could be used to embarrass other people. The sight of Betty's reddening face as she told me her story made me wonder who invented these rules, and why. Did God really care about an apple? I doubted it. The way Waltruda acted toward Betty, who, after all, was merely hungry, horrified me. But I said nothing. I had been bold enough for one day, and I knew my thoughts would not change anything that Waltruda did.

Food endlessly ruled our days. After we spent the morning drilling our classes in math, reading, or spelling, we hurried to the school cafeteria to supervise our students as they ate in the crowded, noisy room. We envied their gooey peanut butter and jelly sandwiches, and secretly laughed at the squashed bananas that the boys used as weapons in their school yard battles.

"Now, eat those bananas," I told them.

"They are good for you," I added in my best preachy tone. I wondered if they knew I laughed when I turned my back on them, and I didn't really care if they had a little fun, as long as Waltruda didn't see me ignoring their shenanigans.

The convent cook, Sister Salvatore, had the entire morning to prepare our own miserable lunch. She sat with her shoes off, and rested her sweaty feet on top of a pile of old wooden egg crates in a corner of her tiny pantry. This was the only place where she could listen to her contraband radio without being discovered by Sister Waltruda, who allowed no one to possess a radio.

When Salvatore heard the school bell ring to end morning classes, she leapt up from her secret listening post and turned the broiler on high. Thus, the hamburgers were always scorched and dried out by the time they were served. If we had betrayed Salvatore's little secret about the radio to the superior, the food would not have changed, so we said nothing. Salvatore yelled when she saw the resident mouse running out of the oven. That was something for which we were grateful! At least the mouse was deterred from nibbling at one of our burgers. If Betty and I could have bargained for more, in return for keeping Salvatore's secret, we would have requested a radio of our own on which we could listen to "Danny Boy," sung by someone with a brogue!

Waltruda piously ate whatever lunch was placed before her.

"She must have a secret stash of food," Betty muttered, one day. "No one could think these hamburgers taste good."

The other sisters drowned the shriveled meat in a sea of ketchup and gulped them down with mouthfuls of Subic's stale bread. Salvatore returned to her pantry and whiled away the afternoon with her Italian tenors until it was time to invent a supper for us. Waltruda never seemed to notice anything strange about the way Salvatore planned the meals. Maybe she thought Salvatore couldn't read English. Maybe she didn't care.

After an endless recitation of Latin prayers every evening, we ate our last meal of the day. While we picked through the serving dishes searching for something edible, we listened to a reader droning on and on about the exploits of a woman saint, Mother Katherine Mahoney, who complained about nothing.

I wondered if she considered it an honor to be thwarted constantly by the local bishop as she tried to open schools in some abandoned muddy plot of land that the Bishop rejected for any other use. I had read that some of the youngsters regularly had to be treated for persistent frost bite. Sister Mahoney's own children were brought to the convent to see her once or twice a year, but turned their backs on her when she entered the room. Her diary, which was found after her death, described her sadness about her children's behavior.

Betty and I could not understand why the Church so highly praised this odd Mahoney woman. In the end, the Vatican even canonized her and placed her statue in a sanctuary built in her honor. My sister, who heard these tales when she visited us, shook her head when we told the story of the way this strange woman stepped over the prone bodies of her children rather than disobey the bishop.

"Was that the way to become a saint?" my sister used to ask us sarcastically.

We privately had the same shocked opinion of St. Mahoney, but we were afraid to admit it. Mother Josepha had challenged our judgments of others every day for two years, so we found it hard to believe that maybe we were right.

We constantly grappled with the stories of an endless array of women who were presented to us as role models. Sometimes they were self-sacrificing nuns who hungered and thirsted only for God.

"Is that supposed to be us?" Imelda muttered.

On other days our role models were married women, who endlessly cared for hordes of children. Occasionally, as an unexpected reward, these women thought they saw Jesus smiling at them from some dark corner of the kitchen.

"Were our mothers praying now and then when we thought they were ironing our clothes and darning the holes in our father's socks?" I quipped. Secretly I, myself, longed for an amazing vision of Jesus, a gentle reward for days of hunger and depression.

Both of these role models sounded warped to us. We found both the pious nuns and the harried mothers, all of them hoping to see Jesus, somehow incredible. The meal that we gulped down was not any more palatable than the women presented for our emulation. They fed neither our bodies nor our souls.

Is it all a sham? I asked myself. *Is it all an effort to make us labor harder and harder, in order to serve others, regardless of the circumstances in which we find ourselves working?*

But then I looked at Liguori, patiently teaching kids in her crowded classroom and still having success with some of them, or I saw Imelda showing Betty how to get the most out of the little first graders who beamed excitedly when they could read a word or two.

I can be like them, I said to myself, and kept on with my lessons and the piano and the organ and the rest of my own exhausting assignment.

These sisters that I am rubbing shoulders with are role models I can relate to, I told myself.

The strange women whose lives Waltruda made us listen to every night were not heroic in my book. They were subservient to harsh husbands, and unfeeling towards their children. Everything they did went counter to what I wanted to be. At least the heroic tales of Maximilian Kolby did not present him as super-human, the way the Mahoney woman and these other women were pictured.

I began to think about some of the stories I read the year before I entered the convent. When I read some booklets I found in the back of the church, I discovered tales about a fictionalized teenager, named St. Peggy of Chicago. Had she been in my high school class, I would have thought she was a bit odd. But at least she was human and lovable, making her blunders on the road to holiness more acceptable. Of course, the priest in the story forever told St. Peggy of Chicago to do the opposite of what I would have suggested. I still felt there was hope for her if she could just avoid some of his advice.

Mother Josepha would have said to me, "Just who are you with your fancy ideas of what other people should do, if they are to be holy?"

I, who wanted so badly to follow the wishes of Jesus, had tried to listen to Mother Josepha, instead of to my friends, or even myself. But the disparity between my thinking and the lives of everyone but St. Peggy seemed monumental. Imitating her appeared to be my only hope for climbing the Mount Everest of holiness.

Relishing the lives of these saints seemed hard, but relishing our food approached the truly impossible. We ate what the cook called "stew," usually a piece of meat floating in an unsavory liquid, with a long tail of fat loosely attached to it. The mere sight of it made my stomach turn. Vegetables were mushy one day and too stringy to chew the next. Once in a while we received a hamburger like Salvatore's lunch time specialty, either "raw on the inside" or nearly inedible because of overcooking.

Sometimes, after our so-called supper, when Betty and I passed the rooms of a few of the more eccentric sisters, we caught a whiff of a delicious odor escaping from their rooms.

"Does that smell like the stew we just gulped down?" Betty would whisper. We rolled our eyes and continued on to bed, hungry as usual. If we had been college girls, we might have knocked on their doors and asked for a bite of what they were cooking, obviously a concoction that never came from Salvatore's kitchen. It would have been brave, indeed, to interrogate them about how they had the nerve to make a second meal in their rooms. But we all were in the convent, and the thought of such boldness never entered our heads. We had a certain innocence born of wanting to be "good nuns."

Once the "stew" or hamburgers had been tried and rejected, six or seven sisters pushed back their chairs and went in a nightly procession to the cereal cupboard and poured out a bowl of cold cereal for themselves. Did the awful meals satisfy Waltruda, or did she have a stash of food in her room? No one questioned her about our miserable food. We instinctively knew that there would be no change no matter what we said.

What happened to feisty Mary? I asked myself when I struggled with hunger. *She used to argue with her father and insist that she was going to work all summer whether he agreed or not. Where did that girl go?*

And what had happened to bossy Betty? She told me how she used to come home from working at her after-school job and order one of her sisters to unroll Betty's nylon stockings that she had worn all day and wash them for her.

"Howls of protest brought my mother to my sister's rescue," Betty said with a glint in her eye, "but it was worth a try!"

What happened to those strong-minded girls who weren't afraid to try anything that came into their minds? Betty and I didn't discuss it. We were still immersed in belonging to Jesus, no matter what it took. We thought loving Him meant we didn't argue with what we were told to do, no matter how stupid or unfair it was. Once in a while, I thought He was trying hard to have us see life in a more open way than this tight line of thinking that we were following.

Occasionally, if Salvatore had an especially good day, with her feet up, listening to Italian operas, she put a small bowl of hard-boiled eggs on our table. Each of us would reach tentatively for an egg, uncomfortable in the knowledge that taking one would deprive someone else, since there were never enough eggs for all of us. Once, Ligouri reached for an egg at the same moment as I did. Our eyes met. She smiled and put it on my plate. The egg comforted me; her smile warmed me. These moments connected us with bonds that lasted forever. When I heard ten years later that Liguori had become very ill and fearful of "meeting her Maker," I wrote to her and reminded her of the night she gave me the last egg in the bowl.

Betty displayed much more bravery than I, in many ways. She found ways to placate our hunger pangs as time went on by doing our own "stealing of food." She discovered a large tin of cookies in the pantry and constantly re-arranged them. We could eat several of them in the course of a week and strategically hide our theft. It gave us something to look forward to. We would have done well in a James Bond movie.

Betty's boldest move was cooking while the other sisters were attending evening devotions at the parish church. She slipped eggs from one of the smelly crates that Salvatore rested her feet on every day. In a few minutes, she transformed the eggs into a delicious omelet, with melted cheese oozing onto the plate. Betty and I would nervously scarf down that wonderful omelet, the likes of which Salvatore probably never had seen.

But we were afraid of everything. Were the odors of something cooking drifting up the stairs to the rooms of those who had not gone to attend devotions at the church? Would the sisters at church come bursting through the door thinking the kitchen was on fire? Two sisters came into the kitchen once and warned us to be careful. They didn't ask for even a small bite of our meal, but they sniffed the air with an expression of remembered indulgence on their thin faces. We had the omelets only a few times, but the memories of Betty's gutsiness stayed with me for a long, long time. That year, life seemed terrible in so many ways, but we made it through. I would not choose to go through it again. It was not normal living, even for a convent.

THE JOY OF TEACHING WINS THE DAY

During the first few weeks of school, as I ate a miserable breakfast I often thought, *What a horrible way to begin my day. Is this going to be my life forever?*

I grabbed my lesson plans and rushed to the school yard, where we all stood like military generals in the places where our classes had been told to assemble.

"Don't smile before Christmas," we had been told when we were given our final directions for teaching those huge classes. We tried to be stern, we really did, but none of us succeeded. It was so much fun to see children again, pushing and elbowing one another because they saw a new teacher. The shy ones edged over to be next to us .The bold ones yelled, "Good morning, Sister," in an effort to win favor and maybe get first chance to wash the blackboards one afternoon. There were a few parents there, probably to get a glimpse of the new teachers. I talked to them, saying, "Good morning," and telling them my own name too. It was so wonderful to have a conversation. I could have talked forever, standing there in the school yard with children all around me, and the comfort of companionship. There was no niggling feeling of breaking an obscure rule that used to confuse me.

I felt free, gloriously free. Something inside of me said, *You can do this if you can just talk to people every day.* It was my first revelation that maybe I really did have a vocation and could live this strange life with a measure of joy.

You haven't made a mistake in entering the convent, after all, I told myself. *It will all work out in the end.* And I suddenly felt peaceful inside.

After a month or so, I realized that I could never be the classroom disciplinarian that I thought a nun should be. The side of me that wanted fun began taking over spontaneously. If I couldn't have fun in the convent, I was determined to have it in the classroom. Imelda cheered me on. Ligouri helped to organize my lessons. Betty chuckled at the methods that I dreamed up, both to keep my own sanity and to give the kids a good time while they learned. Joel and two of the other sisters reminded me that Waltruda didn't care what methods I used as long as the parents were satisfied.

"Just don't let the kids run wild," they all warned me.

"With 53 kids in the classroom, I will be miserable if they are yelling and running around," I responded.

How I would achieve all that I was supposed to do, I had no idea. I just knew that exhausted, hungry, and nervous as I was, somehow I would succeed. Little by little I began applying my new-found system of teaching to the various required subjects.

One day, when a history lesson bored me with its endless dates, I decided on the spur of the moment to change it that very minute into a play with the boys as wild Indians and the girls as brave pioneer women who faced every danger with brainy solutions. I still remember the boys running down the aisle, waving imaginary tomahawks, and thinking to myself, *This is such fun!* I hugged myself with delight when the lesson was over. I could never put on the same play twice because I never knew when boredom would strike again. Of course, we manufactured the dialog on the day of the play and none of us remembered any of the lines the next day. The students went home on a wave of enormous laughter, but they knew I expected them to remember one or two historical facts the next day.

If a geography lesson required what I considered to be too much memorization, I crammed geography facts into familiar tunes that we sang with gusto every morning. The Rhine, the Rhone, the Danube and the Po were as much a part of their musical repertoire as the solemn hymns that I probably should have been teaching them. The beat to the music captured their imagination. When I gave a geography test, I could hear them singing their songs as they scribbled down the names of the rivers.

What a delight this is, I said to myself. *I am so happy.*

If there were poems that they were required to learn, I managed to force them into reciting these great poems every day, with the punctuation included. I knew it spoiled the rhythm of the lines, and sometimes a parent looked a little shocked when they heard my class reciting, "Oh Captain, comma, my captain, exclamation point!" But at least they knew their poetry by the end of the term.

My mother gave me recordings of all the poems that my class studied. I played them as a reward if they learned their punctuation. They used to plead with me to let them hear the poem again, even after the bell rang. I felt so successful. They learned to love poetry, those same glorious poems I had loved all my life. I still felt hungry, I still didn't like praying in Latin, but I thoroughly enjoyed teaching. I loved the kids, they loved me. My life was good! I had so much fun.

When Waltruda decided that the children should learn a "bit of science," as she put it, I told her I didn't know enough science to teach the children more than one or two facts a week. In certain ways, Sister Waltruda was naïve, and I saw that this could work in my favor. I tried the same gambit when I needed to drop some of my piano students; I claimed they had progressed past my level of piano skills. She believed everything I told her about educational subjects. I felt lucky that she was so remiss in training as a teacher, or even as a principal. I was shocked but happy to find that there was such an easy solution for ridding myself of some of the burdens of the extra tasks she had given me. I simply resorted to lying when I desperately needed to get relief from too much work. I could not believe I had become so wily.

I decided to teach mathematics in small groups, with one "good" student responsible for teaching two other students, as I circled the room checking my pseudo teachers. They were calmer than I with their small groups of students, and they didn't yell as much. In fact, the girls I picked to be the mathematics helpers glowed with pride as they helped their less able friends. I used to wonder if, in later years, a few of those students went on to be teachers. I always praised the "new teachers," and their "students" were pleased not to be always failing in their math lessons.

I taught "by the seat of my pants," scrambling for ways to help the students that I was responsible for. There was one embarrassing instance when I drilled into the heads of my fourth graders that 6 x 7 equaled 49.

Child after child, the next day, reminded me, "Sister, my mother said to tell you that 6 x 7 equals 42." Since I had more than 50 children in the class, it was humiliating when the same refrain was repeated by almost every child in the class as they marched past me into the classroom. I longed to yell, "Shut up," but of course I couldn't. The parents probably just thought I made a simple mistake. They had no idea that my brain had turned to mathematical mush trying to remember numbers, tables, and where to put the decimal points.

Teaching about religion was somewhat of a failure in my classroom. No matter how hard I tried I could not convince my students to attend daily Mass like the other students piously did. I think they knew that I really didn't care whether or not they dragged themselves to church during the week, although a few faithful souls went day after day.

When I thought I really would be embarrassed by their poor attendance, I pleaded with them to attend on a certain day when the monsignor would be celebrating some feast day or other. They usually piled into the pews on those occasions. The boys gave me a grin and the girls acted as if they really wanted to be there and had longed for an excuse to come. I wondered if they thought they should go to Mass because it pleased me, or because there was a higher purpose in my pleas to them to attend. Truthfully, I simply wanted them to have something to hang onto in the midst of life's trials.

In the middle of the confusion and exhaustion of those first years of teaching, something good happened for me. I became joyful. If I could have bottled my joy, I would have made a fortune, doling out appropriate portions to the needy as if I were some kind of traveling salesperson with a strange new potion designed to cure frightening diseases of the soul.

Come here for your dose of how to be happy. But of course it was much more than that. There was something good going on that I never understood both in myself and in the parish.

When I tried to figure it out with Imelda, she grinned at me, and said, "It's love, Mary. Even with all the hunger and aggravation from various sources, there is still enough caring going on here to balance out the rage that we are all feeling. I can't explain it any better than that."

Then with a twinkle in her eye, she added, "It's humor too, Mary. If you don't laugh, you'll cry. Your sense of humor will pull you through, just when you think you are going to scream."

She knows me, I thought. I didn't feel less hungry or tired, but somehow I was more relaxed in the core of my being.

The people in the parish were mostly poor and had lots of troubles. But by their own struggles in the lives they were leading, they inspired us, and humbled us. They did not understand our lives or our vows any more than our parents did. We who had made these vows at such a young age probably did not understand them either. In some strange way, the parish and the sisters helped one another, soothed and comforted each other. We all moved on in our lives unaware of what was going on but somehow we knew that something good was happening in each of us. Like all things spiritual, we felt but could not explain it. We knew only that some kind of rebirth was taking place in our souls, and for that we were deeply grateful.

BETTY AND MARY DISCOVER THAT CONVENT LIFE IS NOT ALL BAD

B etty and I became best buddies during our first few years of teaching in that old convent with its eccentric superior and its impossible classroom assignments.

Sister Waltruda quickly decided that I was too valuable as a money-maker for the convent to give me any more assignments. As a result Betty was designated as the shopper/laundress/nurse if needed/in addition, of course, to teacher of almost a hundred first graders. The convent rule at that time required that no sister walked outside alone. Betty, who already served in so many capacities, became the permanent companion for the almost daily shopping sprees of the Superior.

My own companion was always someone carelessly assigned by Sister Waltruda, without regard to our personal affection, or lack thereof, for each other. Such a consideration probably never entered her mind.

One of my least favorite companions was Sister Albertina, who manufactured a coughing fit if I asked her a question, then smiled politely when her phony spasm was over. She motioned to her throat as a way of warding off any more conversation for the rest of the walk. I felt like yelling at her and walking off in a huff until she uttered at least one little syllable. Her silence infuriated me.

One time I conducted an experiment as I sat opposite her during a feast day dinner, when we were allowed to talk. I started a conversation with her, but to no avail. She took a mouthful of potato or meat, and spent the rest of the meal chewing slowly, pointing to her mouth frequently and smiling politely as if to say, "I can't speak until I swallow this food." Then she spent the rest of the meal managing not to speak to me or to anyone else at the table.

Since we were allowed to talk freely when we were outside the convent, I tried to accept being assigned this silent companion as a penance for some forgotten sin in my past. It was a stretch, even for me, "Little Miss Pious," as my sister used to call me at home, to try to think of some God-ordained reason. Maybe I had gossiped too much when I was younger, so now I had to keep silence when I could have been chatting.

Chance never seemed to play a role in my life at that time. It seemed that God always arranged what was going on in an effort to teach me some lesson that apparently I had resisted learning. I struggled to make up reasons why things happened in my life, and somehow it was always because I had failed at some point in my past and needed reminders.

* * * * *

Sister Irmgard, my regularly assigned companion, was a much older sister. She made loud, embarrassing references to digestive problems as we walked along.

"My lower story is bothering me today," she whined, pointing to her abdomen, as we walked along.

Nothing could divert her from loudly detailing all her embarrassing symptoms no matter how much I blushed.

Lost in her own world of life's difficulties, she was convinced that no one cared about her. I knew that nothing could divert her from the pleasurable activity of feeling sorry for herself.

Even the splash of yellow forsythia blossoms at the corner of our convent wall gave her a forum for more moaning. I felt immediately sorry each time that I pointed them out to her.

"Only three lousy blossoms," she said in her whiny monotone, and I gave up. I wanted to break off three or four of those lovely flowers for her, and force them gently into her hands. I wanted her to carry them peacefully for the rest of the walk. I ached to hear her say they were beautiful, beautiful like all of God's creation. I hated our walks. They were bringing out anger in me, mixed with guilt. Why wasn't I nicer to her? Why wasn't I acting like St. Therese, who forced herself to use each occasion when she was upset or hurting as a chance to become more devoted to Jesus?

I had no answer. All I wanted was a normal conversation with someone. Was it really so much to ask?

I wondered if Irmgard realized how annoying I found her during our obligatory walks together. I knew only that she made a point to march up the chapel aisle every morning to wake me up as I slumped over my prayer bench with my head bobbing in undignified slumber. She would hiss into my ear, "Wake up!" and clomp back to her prayer bench. Some of the other sisters in that convent didn't notice (or care) how tired I seemed. They just wanted me to be like them, upright and praying. Maybe she was "getting even" with me for not giving her enough sympathy when she complained. I never asked her. I probably didn't want to know.

In my quiet moments, while I waited for Sister Waltruda to assign my companion for a trip to the store, I thought, *Will it be the one who can't even have a decent conversation, or the one whose heart doesn't lift at the sight of yellow forsythias?*

Betty and I often spoke privately about the ironic fact that there was no restriction on the number of students that could be packed into your classroom, where there was much greater possibility of murder or mayhem being committed than there was of any shenanigans being conducted if a lone sister strolled by herself to the corner and back just for a change of environment. Add to this that any time we walked outside, we were forbidden to glance at the dresses or coats in the store windows as we passed by them, or even to comment on the pretty outfit that a woman walking towards us wore. Should we fail in these regards, our nervous consciences obliged us to confess to the superior that we had been talking about such a vain thing as clothing, or heaven

A sensitive person, with real Irish wit, Betty was a wonderful story-teller. She had not a trace of meanness in her and was as sincere as she was good. Her stories of Sister Waltruda and the shopping sprees were real, and so was Betty.

Betty's stints as laundress were at least not in the public eye, since they involved only the laundry of Sister Waltruda. The old woman changed her underwear only once a week. Betty would run down the stairs to the laundry room clutching Waltruda's malodorous underwear with one hand and holding her nose with the other.

"Mary," she would whisper to me later. "I felt so sorry for you when I ran past the piano room. You were asleep with your head on your chest while your piano student was banging away on the piano, and I couldn't help you." Then Betty hurried into the laundry room with its rows of deep metal sinks and its soap dishes containing slivers of old soap balanced precariously near the rusty pipes. Betty did her best to cling to the slippery slivers of old brown soap, skinning her knuckles in her efforts to scrub Waltruda's heavy mohair habit.

Once the habit had been laboriously scrubbed, Betty put the heavy garment through an old-fashioned wooden wringer that could service only one or two items at a time. Ligouri caught her crying once from pure exhaustion and disgust. The old patched underwear still waited to be washed, along with a few sticky hankies. The two of them worked together on the miserable task until Waltruda's clothing had lost its distasteful odors. The outer garments had to be ironed using a heavy old-fashioned monstrosity of an iron. "Shopping" and teaching had already depleted most of Betty's energy, leaving her with only the hope of a nap during evening meditation.

There was nothing easy about life for Betty or for me in that old convent, but the relief of seeing our friends at Normal School on Saturdays boosted our spirits and raised our sights to a better world awaiting us in a life without Waltruda.

"After all, she could always be transferred, couldn't she?" we would say hopefully to each other. As we struggled with teaching huge classes, Imelda and Ligouri strengthened us with ideas on teaching and the gift of laughing at things that we would not have seen as funny in another setting. Despite Waltruda's peculiarities, we were semi-happy. The talents that the novitiate crushed in me began to come to life again. I made five -foot high drawings of Jesus, Mary and a worn-out looking St. Joseph to paste onto my classroom windows at Christmas. My mother brought tiny individual gifts for each child in my class, which thrilled me. A blotter finally covered my old-fashioned classroom desk and hid its splintery wooden top. I almost began to feel like a normal human being. Most of all, the delight of being with children, playing with them, (and of course, being able to escape from them when the day was over), gave me a sense that life was not over for me yet.

The abundant food we had both hoped for when we left the novitiate was not ours, but the comradeship of some talented, humorous sisters comforted us. We learned to ignore the odd ones. We struggled along. We never felt as if Jesus had abandoned us. We just couldn't figure out where He had gone, but we were comfortable with the substitutes for Him whom we found around us. It began to feel okay, still weird, not great, but approaching what a convent would call okay. Now if we could just get a decent meal… and get rid of some of these rules… and… and… and..! I stuttered when I tried to think of the future. "I'll figure it out as I go along," I said to myself blithely, with the optimism of youth. And so I did.

SUMMERTIME AND THE LIVING IS EASY

A s the months wore on and the end of school approached, we heard rumors of summer assignments that Sister Waltruda would announce to us in June. We might be sent to a summer camp for girls located in a beautiful mountain area in Sullivan County, New York. One possibility was that we would serve as camp counselors. The other assignment was of a more humble nature. We could spend several hours each day piling up dirty dishes in the camp kitchen and loading them into a clunky old dishwasher that was prone to breaking down.

As it turned out, Betty and I both were assigned to the camp kitchen. We packed our suitcases and managed to get rides with two sisters from a nearby convent. They had an old blue convertible, and as soon as we passed the city limits, Sister Ann ,who was one of our pals from high school, rolled back the cloth top of the car. Suddenly, our veils billowed and blew like sails on a ship. We were beyond thrilled. It was our first taste of freedom since the day we entered the convent. Those wildly-flying veils said it all.

When we reached St. Joseph's Camp, Ann discreetly closed the top of the car, and we drew up outside a rather large white building with a simple sign saying "St. Dominic's Villa." Through the half-open door, we could hear loud laughter and yelps of excited greetings.

"Is this our summer home?" I said to Betty. We could hardly believe our luck. And there was more to come! Inside that blessed villa, there was no rule of silence. We could talk all night long if we wanted, provided that we managed to get up for Mass each morning and met our work obligations in the camp kitchen. Our Latin prayers still had to be recited, but on our own time, not in a muddled group leaning against uncomfortable prayer benches. And even though we

119

were assigned to specific areas in the Villa, with only two-in-a-room, we were allowed to wander into other rooms anytime we wanted and lie on the beds, or sit on the floor, talking, sharing gossip and discussing problems in our lives. Sometimes there were five and six sisters in one room, laughing and chatting like we used to do at home. Our letters and phone calls were uncensored. We ate camp food! Our parents could come to visit us whenever we were not working. We could sit on the lawn with whomever we chose and eat ice-cream cones like we did in the old days when we were carefree teenagers, toying with dreams of becoming nuns someday. Suddenly we felt beautifully alive again, even if we knew that this freedom would be ours for only a few summer months.

The most amazing part of all that summer was that we, so young and inexperienced, were welcomed as celebrities by all the sisters, even the ones that we had never met before. Everyone wanted to hear stories about Sister Waltruda, the shopping sprees, the laundry, the food, our midnight omelets, our cookie shifting, our walks to Normal School, the huge class sizes, the cracked eggs, the spotted fruit, the mange cure for dandruff, the Christmas shopping, everything and anything connected with our winter residence, as they referred to it. They were agog at our stories, and listened to the same tales over and over, hooting and hollering when we reached the conclusions. We were not unkind. We told the truth, which—as Ripley said—was stranger than fiction. We reminded each other of some of the details when the rush of the story tripped us up in the telling. This was our entrance into the world of drama and we loved it! We had earned our place in the spotlight.

The work in the camp kitchen was long, hot and burdensome, but we ate before the campers, so we had energy to meet our obligations. When we finally finished, we would lie around on the old wooden docks by the lake, take a swim and drag ourselves onto another larger dock where we would try to get a tan.

"Always remember," the old-timers would remind us, "This is a man-made lake, and the bottom is all mud, with water-snakes gliding around. Don't put your feet down."

So I would take huge breaths when I started swimming and arrive red-faced and gasping at the dock where my friends were lolling about. Sometimes we were even allowed to use the row-boats, and we propelled one another around as if we were characters in a Scott Fitzgerald story of millionaires on Long Island Sound where the water was pristine and there were no snakes to trouble our toes.

By nightfall we had finished our third round of dish-washing, and met with our friends again, or greeted some new ones. We walked up to the grotto of the Virgin Mary, which was about a half-mile up a winding hill, and said the rosary on the way up. I never liked the rosary so I just walked up quietly, listening to the other sisters murmuring their Hail Mary's while I fingered my big black rosary beads just to be a part of it all.

If we were still ready to chat for a while, there was always someone to talk to, but usually by the end of the day we were eager to go to bed, thankful for a peaceful day.

Toward the end of the summer, we noticed that some of the campers and even a few of the sisters were rather lethargic. We attributed it to hot weather and hard work. Then a fearsome announcement was made one morning, two weeks before camp was scheduled to officially close. For some reason, everything was closing down early, with no tangible explanation given. Slowly details slipped out.

One rumor said that the doctor who had cleared the youngsters to attend camp had been professionally careless in screening for contagious diseases and several of the girls had hepatitis. Another blamed impurities in the water supply. Regardless of the cause of the outbreak, all the campers were sent home immediately with instructions to their parents about their care. The camp grounds were shut down while more and more rumors flew. A doctor hired by the convent was required to give hepatitis tests to the sisters who had been losing energy. They found, to our distress, that several of those who had been staying in the Villa were suffering from hepatitis as well. They were shunted off without so much as a chance to say goodbye to us, their comrades, and deposited in an old age home, managed by our sisters.

The home was in a beautiful, but isolated area of Long Island, where we had no access to our friends for the better part of a year. We could only imagine the loneliness they endured, without a letter or phone call. Dribs and drabs of information reached us over the great divide of convent rules but the warmth of our beautiful summer days vanished along with the hepatitis. It was a desperately lonely time for all of us, thinking of them and praying for them, but deprived of their familiar voices and even their complaints, which we would have been so glad to share if that sharing would have been a comfort to them. Eventually, they recovered but not until many months had passed. Their long convalescence was a gloomy period in our lives.

Betty and I returned to our convent quickly and began our regular schedule of teaching along with all our chores. There was a difference in us, however, after that wonderful summer. We had tasted what it meant to think for ourselves, even though we were still in the convent. We had lost a bit of our slavish obedience to all the philosophies that had entangled our minds while we were in the novitiate and which we had desperately tried to maintain all during our first year of teaching. We were still sisters. We would be sisters for many more years. But a measure of balance had edged its way into our thinking and would continue to strengthen us as we continued to mature as young women and as sisters.

Weekly bulletins came into our convent via rumors at Normal School about the spread of the hepatitis among the sisters who had worked at camp during the summer. Every week one or two more sisters showed signs of hepatitis, and we lived in dread that more of our friends would show up on the list. Finally the numbers dwindled and we knew that the spread of the disease was over.

Sister Waltruda Becomes Gravely Ill

About that time, Sister Waltruda began to look peculiar to us. She was not only lethargic. She had a decidedly yellow cast to her skin and a change in her eye-color. This was not camp where we could force her to go to a camp doctor. We were in the convent where most things were utterly beyond our control. We began to avoid the communal bathroom that she used. We had no idea how hepatitis was transmitted but we knew that it had spread somehow at the camp. In the usual way of the young, we were focused on our own health, despite the daily suggestion that perhaps what was wrong with Sister Waltruda had nothing to do with the illness that had spread among the sisters who had been at camp with us.

Our Polish superior came from what our parents referred to as "the old country," where doctors used old-fashioned techniques and parents usually provided the most useful systems of allaying illnesses. But this was not the "old country" and some of our friends had contracted hepatitis while we were all at camp, and Sister Waltruda was growing more yellow with each passing day. True to form, she decided that Betty should take her to a leech doctor, somewhere in Brooklyn, where leeches could be applied to her face.

Betty obediently found a way to get Sister Waltruda to this doctor. He applied leeches to her face until they had sucked the blood from the poor woman's body and supposedly administered their ancient cure. She came home looking like a ghost, with not a trace of color in her face. Two small black dots on her temples betrayed the spots where the leeches had been at work. A few more treatments and Sister Waltruda felt sure she would no longer have that yellow hue. In the meantime, the pastor became alarmed. He called her a few times. She told him the leech treatment was taking away the yellow color, but added with a tinge of fear that her "ureene" was black. As she sat in her usual place in the refectory, picking at that miserable food, we felt more and more hysterical. Her yellow color became terribly pronounced. The leech doctor decided that Betty should buy a mustard plaster from the druggist and apply it to Sister Waltruda's back. Other patients with the same malady had been helped by this remedy when the leeches had not managed to return the patient's color permanently to a healthy pallor. Betty read all the directions and carefully placed the plaster on the poor woman's back, to no avail.

One of the older sisters in the convent, who usually stayed out of things, decided that something had to be done, and secretly called a local doctor who demanded that Sister Waltruda be seen immediately at a well-respected hospital nearby. She was taken there early the next morning, and was dead from liver cancer in two days.

We were terribly shocked at her sudden death. The poor woman struggled along, tried remedies from "the old country," insisted on leeches and mustard plasters, and had not asked for anything special from anyone. All along, we thought that she had hepatitis and lived in dread that, if we contracted it ourselves, we would find ourselves hustled out to that far-away rest home for recuperation. Like most young people, we were self-centered. We never dreamed that this old woman who never complained had liver cancer.

Betty and I had to go to the hospital to identify the body. The doctor gave us a cursory examination because of the hepatitis scare at the camp where we had worked all summer. Cleared of any infection, we returned to the convent. Betty, who was only twenty years old, dressed the body after the mortuary had prepared Waltruda for burial. It seemed impossible to shed tears for Waltruda. We had never felt really close to her. She was too odd and had imposed too many restrictions on us in an already restricted world. We had never hated her, but we didn't love her either.

In her own gruff way, Waltruda was vaguely kind, but she was too tied to convent rules to show an understanding of our feelings.

Sometimes, weak traces of a long-smothered tenderness showed itself. She used to call Betty "Little One." Once, when I asked Betty why Sister Waltruda called her by that term, she said that she was the youngest one in the convent; that was where the term, "Little One" came from. One other time, when we had been in Holy Angels Convent for only a few weeks, Betty—who was devoted to St. Francis, a long-ago saint who loved the down-trodden— invited two of the vagrants who came to the convent door to come into the parlor, where she had them sit down and provided them with sandwiches. Sister Waltruda's shouts, when she saw the disreputable looking vagrants in our parlor, sent them out, complete with their sandwiches.

The custom in that convent was to celebrate the feast day of the superior with some kind of home-made gifts, no matter how untalented we were. In the case of Sister Waltruda's feast day, we decided to make a facsimile of a rosary, since we had nothing else to give her. A few of us got a hole-puncher, and a large piece of white typing paper, and we hole-punched fifty holes, which Imelda arranged in the form of an immense rosary arranged on the community room table.

Sister Waltruda thanked us so proudly. She thought we had cut out the little white circles by hand, and took it as a sign of our caring for her. We were embarrassed that she could have supposed that we had personally cut out those pseudo rosary beads by hand and suddenly didn't want her to know that we had used the hole-puncher to make them. We smiled at her innocent pleasure that day, and to our surprise realized that she was a simple soul who occasionally wanted some small proofs of caring from others.

Now that she was gone to a "better place," as all the holy books said, we were far more concerned with what would happen to us, now that we would be getting a new superior, than we were with anything else. It sounds cold when I think about it, but it was the way it was.

She had been like a Dickens character, and we spent our time fantasizing about our next superior rather than bemoaning her loss. As the old Irish saying went, "Waltruda, we hardly knew ye."

According to the convent customs, the body of Sister Waltruda was laid out in the convent parlor on a sturdy table that Betty had covered with a clean cloth. Several chairs for mourners were arranged at the foot of the body. Following convent custom, Betty placed a transparent veil over Sister Waltruda's face and twined an old rosary that she found lying under the desk in Waltruda's bedroom around the dead woman's fingers. It was a strange and solemn time for all of us. After a day, she was transported to our cemetery in Amityville, and buried there.

At the gravesite that chilly February day we chanted the prayer for the deceased, the "De Profundis" that we had learned while we were in the novitiate. "Out of the depths, Oh Lord," our quavering voices reminded Him, "If You mark our iniquities, who among us could stand?" We had not dreamed that we would be praying such a poignant prayer together at the grave of our first superior less than two years after our arrival at the convent. There were no tears among us, only the solemn feeling that one gets at any death when mortality forces itself on us, regardless of our age.

On the day following the burial, all of Waltruda's personal belongings were arranged on the large community room table. We were told we could take anything we wanted. The oldest sisters in the convent had first choice of her pitiful belongings.

There were a few Polish-language prayer books, a small rosary, a pair or two of thickly-darned stockings, and her woolen shawl which she wrapped around her shoulders even when she was sitting at her desk. The underwear that Betty had so carefully washed, and her mohair habit with threadbare sections that were ready for darning were folded neatly for anyone to take. Anything that was not claimed by the sisters was given to the poor. There was nothing there that I wanted. It reminded me of the story in the Christmas Carol when all of Scrooge's belongings were grabbed up by people that hardly knew him and did not care whether he was alive or dead. Our leave-taking of Sister Waltruda was not as stark as the Dickens story but in our souls there was hardly an acknowledgement that another human being had passed on. We finished our final obligatory prayers for the "eternal rest" of her soul, and waited with a secret excitement for our new superior to enter our lives. We wondered selfishly why God couldn't have given us the rest of the summer before illness and death forced their way into our lives.

A NEW SUPERIOR AND KIND OF A NEW LIFE

It did not take long for us to see that Sister Olympia had a more casual attitude toward the convent rules that we had been struggling with for almost four years now. We were still bound by long hours of silence, but if she came upon us chatting quietly in the community room when we were supposedly preparing our lesson plans for the following day, breaking silence was not a cause célèbre necessitating a penance. A mild frown was sufficient to remind us that we were still in the convent. We felt a little guilty on those occasions, as if we had betrayed her trust.

Just because she allows us to have beer once in a while at supper, I said to myself, *doesn't mean she's willing to let us break some of the rules.*

Monastic penances had been a regular part of our lives in the novitiate. Now we told "Do you remember?" stories about them and winced when we recalled how hard we tried to make sense of them, in this twentieth century life of ours.

"They're pieces of our lives now," Betty and I reminded each other. "They are signs of our becoming real nuns."

In the novitiate, the penances had been part of the comradeship growing by leaps and bounds among the gaggle of teenagers who were becoming sisters in the true sense of the word. These strange practices were meant to train us to adhere to the ancient customs of the convent. Instead they embarrassed us, or made us want to giggle. Sometimes our reactions, as we reluctantly followed Mother Josepha's directions, surprised us and we found ourselves bound to each other in a new way as we stumbled through the age-old penances. I wondered if Mother Josepha knew that would happen.

One day we remembered the day Mother Josepha decided Betty and I had forgotten the real purpose of our monastic rules and ordered us to kiss the feet of the superiors at the head table during dinner as a reminder of why we were in the convent. We knew we couldn't say "No," so the two of us, blushing wildly, slid on our stomachs under the long refectory table kissing one black-shod foot after another while the owners slurped their soup or picked at their salads. As I edged my way from foot to foot, one kindly sister gently pushed her foot nearer to my flushed face to help me to finish my penance sooner. I longed to say, "Thank you" to her for that loving gesture.

What a dear old soul she is, I whispered to myself. In another life, I would have hugged her. In this silent, suppressed life, I didn't even know her name, but I loved her all the same.

Another time, Mother Josepha gave me a hair shirt to wear, probably mistaking my nervousness for saintly intensity. I had been madly flattered that day.

I'm moving on in the parade of penances, I told myself. *Perhaps I will be a saint after all. How I wish I could tell all my friends. How jealous they would be!* But she only allowed me to wear my hair-shirt for a single day. Maybe I had been unworthy of wearing it any longer. I was embarrassed to ask her. At least I had been singled out once for a special penance.

If Sister Olympia had known how skewed our thinking had been only a few years ago, she would have shaken her head. As it was, she ignored most of our transgressions, and resurrected very few of the old penances. I was not exactly sorry to see them go. They were part of our history, even if they were not used as often anymore. In my heart, I was still loyal to them in a secret sort of way.

They were, after all, a link to a shadowy past and even though I may not have wanted to perform them as frequently as we did in the early days of the novitiate, I wanted them to be available if needed. My convent memories would have lost something, the link to other centuries, the faint connection to part of another life. It was a fragment of a pattern, in a life I didn't want to see swept bare of traditions.

But now, in my new world without Waltruda's unpredictable rules, I wanted as much freedom as Sister Olympia could manage to give us. If she opened the door to too many freedoms, she might have gotten a surprise visit from Reverend Mother and been bundled off for a review of the Holy Rule. Juggling the convent customs according to her own interpretation, would be a delicate balance for her.

Luckily for us, she had a sense of fun, giving us beer at some meals, treating us with German bratwurst, and in short making our lives pleasant with simple things. She managed to make the convent a place we already knew, with grating as well as subtle restrictions. But she wasn't Waltruda with her strange methods of governing us. The scary Holy Rule that had given me the shivers for several years was becoming less of a tyrant. More, I couldn't ask for.

A Sweet Christmas Story

As Christmas drew near, I longed for more spontaneity in my life and so I asked Olympia if I could celebrate that favorite holiday of mine in a special way. I had only been in the convent a few years and was still learning the ropes, so to speak. Everything was still new to me and even ways of celebrating festivities like Christmas seemed almost too religious, too forced in their gaiety. At odd moments I thought back to my mother whose approach to Christmas was incredibly natural and gloriously spontaneous. I missed it—and her.

It was because of this that I began thinking of ways to bring a spark of newness into the convent celebrations. Several miles away from our convent, there was a home for retired sisters, old, fragile and in some instances, mentally unstable. They were German, like most of our sisters at that time, since the original founders were from Ratisbon. I had seen pictures of them, looking solidly fixed in their setting—fed with heavy Germanic food, clothed in their white habits the same as ours, their veils askew, and their rosary beads dangling from their thick leather belts. Some of them looked bored; others seemed sad. I wondered if there was anything interesting in their lives.

I was teaching fourth grade, and loving it. Our school was situated in an impoverished immigrant setting where very few parents spoke English and children were struggling to adjust to two different cultures. But the parents trusted me and were usually willing to follow my lead in extracurricular activities. They were accustomed to having foreign languages swirling around them; so why not have their own children learn "Silent Night" in German, taught by me, an Irish girl who had never spoken that language in my life. Besides, having these bright-eyed fourth graders sing in German for the nuns at the retirement home might enliven Christmas both for me and for the old nuns as well. Sister Ligouri, whose grandmother came from Bavaria, volunteered to practice the proper pronunciation of those strange syllables with me, until I could lead my excited choir without too many glaring mistakes.

So why not! Sister Olympia let me steal some minutes every day to teach the fourth graders that lovely old Christmas carol. The pastor paid for the bus. The Superior at the old home sent a list of simple gifts that we could bring. We wrapped them during the reading class. We fastened bows on top of the meager presents, our eyes glowing. Best of all, my mother donated a table-top tree, complete with decorations, to bring on our Christmas safari.

The day came... the bus was late... phone calls were made... the bus came. We were so excited we could hardly breathe. We practiced our singing on the bus. When we reached the shuttered convent, I allowed one of the taller children to bang the old-fashioned knocker wildly until we could hear someone inside that mammoth building calling, "Coming, coming." And then the door opened, and a plump, red-faced nun began laughing and crying all at once. "We were afraid you weren't coming," she blubbered, and wiped her face with an old hanky. We followed her, tripping over the rag rugs, lugging my mother's Christmas tree, and at last gathering in the family room at the old home.

Thirty ancient sisters sat in a circle, in the center of which we placed my precious tree. The few gifts were piled in a pathetic arrangement. The grand moment came. My ragamuffin choristers began singing "Silent Night" in German. Suddenly a glorious surprise burst out, one I could never have planned. The old German sisters began singing in the guttural language of their childhood, filling the simple room with the sounds of the ancient hymn. Some sisters cried and held their shaking hands out to us. I touched their knobby fingers gently, and the children shyly did the same. We smiled at one another and sang the hymn a second time, not wanting to end the beautiful moment so soon. The children reveled at the success of their Christmas singing, and so did I.

As we left, I scooped up my mother's little tree, and held it carefully so its decorations would remain intact. Two sisters hobbled after us, calling in wavering voices, "Aren't you leaving the tree?" "Of course, "I said. I really didn't want to. It had been my mother's gift to me after all.

But I left it, and the strains of the Silent Night remained with me. It is one of the loveliest Christmas memories I have.

RULES, REGULATIONS, AND REBELLIONS

The Council held meetings at the Motherhouse every two years. Betty and I decided that only humorless superiors were allowed to be part of those somber gatherings. Decisions made in the past burdened us with ever more dismal regulations, while daily reminders of the holiness of tradition made us too anxious to ask that anything be changed. Only when we walked over to the school, or ironed altar cloths in the laundry room, were we more outspoken. We were not afraid of each other. Those were the times when we complained angrily to one another through gritted teeth. Sometimes we dreamed blissfully of being taken into the decision making process, which we correctly saw as the way to greater leniency.

A little break in the secrecy that surrounded the deliberations of the superiors suddenly came a few years after we made our first vows. Two great things happened. First of all, Betty, Imelda, Ligouri, and I were left alone in the convent for an entire week while Sister Olympia attended the Council meeting in the Motherhouse. Sister Cunegunda, an old sister left in charge of us wild young things, showed only a vague interest in supervising us. She rang the bell in the early morning for us to say our prayers, and then left us to our own devices for the rest of the day. We mumbled the daily psalms quickly and then relaxed in the community room, chatting about our classes, reminiscing about our families, and eating whatever we could find in the pantry.

"At least we can throw out what we don't want," Betty said cheerfully, tossing some moldy bread.

The best part of all was feeling free from the decisions of the Superior about how we spent our time that week. It was a delightful change from the rigid regulations that usually formed our days, even with Sister Olympia who tried to give us easy times whenever she could.

"Imagine living like this all the time," I said to Betty and Imelda.

"Free as birds," Imelda replied, a twinkle in her eye. "Let's take a walk to Our Lady of Czestochowa Church," she suggested.

"Oh no!" we groaned. "All we ever heard about when we lived with Sister Waltruda were the miracles that Our Lady of Czestochowa performed in Poland, and how fortunate we were to have a book about her in the convent library."

"Imelda, they were written in Polish, remember?" I reminded her with a giggle. "Anyhow, it is too far to walk and none of us have carfare to get there. Maybe we can take a stroll to the corner and look at the clothes in the store windows."

That was our adventure for the day. The four of us rejoiced in the sheer boldness of it. Walking where we wanted and making believe that we had money to buy something! Even the luxury of choosing our own walking companions was exciting. We were like teenagers, bursting with that special delight that comes when you are on the cusp of being on your own.

Just when we were counting down the days that were left in our week, a phone call came from the Motherhouse where all the superiors were still huddled together making up new rules for us to hate. Betty burst into the community room where we had been holed up planning our next adventure before the superior came home to spoil it all.

"Listen, everybody," she yelled. "Sister Olympia left a message with Cunegunda last night. She wants to know if there are any changes in convent rules that we'd like her to submit to the Council for a vote."

"There's no chance that any of our ideas will be accepted," I said to Liguori, but I hurried to find my pen and pad of yellow paper anyway and began writing madly.

I noticed that Sister Cunegunda didn't share in our activity. "I like things just the way they are," she grunted, and settled into her rocking chair, her eyes closed, apparently determined to ignore the hub-bub around her.

The next day, we were frenzied, calling across to one another with our ideas and crossing out bolder suggestions lest their very brazenness betray our true thoughts in case someone outside the convent walls should find them in the trash. Finally, we were finished. We gathered our papers, with their scribbled suggestions, crossed-out, re-numbered, and underlined in red. Each of us read our list to our little group, feeling as if we had graduated from kindergarten to be with the big guys, part of the ruling body, so to speak.

We looked at one another in embarrassment when we heard only one request repeated on each list. It was not for better food, not to see our parents more often, not even for an increase in our meager monthly allowance. We wanted only one thing, and that was to exchange our bulky nightgowns for pajamas. If only we could sleep unencumbered by swaths of nightgown material when the day was over! It sounded like a dream come true.

What was the most unlikely reason why the Superiors were so stubborn about keeping the old-fashioned rules about night clothes in full force? The famous play, "Fiddler on the Roof" screamed the answer. TRADITION! Here we were, young women, battling the mindset of superiors who insisted that we wear nightgowns. They wanted our nightgowns to remind us of the long white robes that Dominic, our founder, wore centuries ago as he tramped through muddy pathways and preached to anyone who would listen to his revolutionary ideas. Like our superiors, we too longed to have Dominic's single-mindedness in bringing truth to both ourselves and to others. We loved him for his bravery when he struggled daily, as we all did, to be straightforward, when we met obstacles to honesty in our decisions. But wearing nightgowns was not the only way to be faithful to his tenets.

For a moment, as I scribbled my vote for pajamas, I wondered a little guiltily when my old lady nightgowns had stopped reminding me of Dominic's fidelity. Wasn't that the important part of the clothing? Or had it been buried in a wish for greater comfort?

We asked Sister Cunegunda for a big manila envelope and a few stamps and got permission to hurry to the post office before evening prayers to mail our grand ideas to the Motherhouse. We felt excited and nervous. We were thinking independently about the rules in our lives, stating our feelings in writing, like a genteel Declaration of Independence to our higher superiors. We signed our names for all to see, and waited anxiously for a reply to our bold request. None came.

Three days later, on the last day of the Council, our superior called to speak to Sister Cunegunda.

"Tell the sisters that the Motherhouse has rejected their request to wear pajamas to bed. They are to continue to don their traditional nightgowns." Our initial feelings of insult by not being answered directly passed quickly.

"We have crossed the Rubicon," Betty chortled. "The die is cast."

That is how we began carrying the banner for choosing our own bedclothes. Every two years when the month of the bi-yearly council approached, we persevered with our civil barrage about pajamas versus nightgowns. What Betty indelicately called "The Pajama Wars" raged on for four years. Each side sensed that something important transpired in the midst of this ever so genteel argument over what we wore to bed.

Finally, a few "council years" later, a terse announcement was posted on the bulletin board near the community room. It said simply "Those who want pajamas may ask for them only if their nightgowns are no longer serviceable." We balled our nightgowns into tidy bundles and deposited them into the battered dust-bin near the local funeral parlor. We had won the battle. Goliath had succumbed to David at last.

The old nuns continued to wear their white nightgowns; the young nuns donned pajamas, blue, yellow, even a gaudy red. The convent walls were beginning to crumble. Maybe the superiors were right after all. Little things did mean a lot.

VACATION — MORE OR LESS

When I lived at home, I always knew a few months ahead of time where my parents planned to take the family on vacation. Part of the fun was thinking about it. My parents sat at the kitchen table and talked about spending a month at the beach, and which of their many friends would meet us there and for how long. My mother would roll her eyes when the two of them talked about the "how long" part of the month. One year, as a tease, my father decided not to tell his buddies where he had rented a bungalow, but the friends wandered up and down every street until they caught a glimpse of my mother hanging out the wash and the secret was out. My father had to dash out for beer and cold cuts, and my mother ordered him to buy cheap paper plates. My sister and I became instant raconteurs, telling anyone who would listen how we had almost drowned that day when the waves pulled us out beyond the breakers. We shouted fearfully until the waves hurled us back to the shore where we fell gasping on the sand, proud of our prowess in escaping from that wild water.

That year my sister could not persuade my father to let her take time off from her job so she could have more time sashaying along the shoreline waiting for the boys to give a few piercing whistles as she wiggled past, slim and pretty in the bathing suit my mother had bought for her in Bly's Discount Store. My sister and I secretly felt that the old guy, who had owned the store for almost fifty years, should have been paying us just to walk through the door, giving him some free advertisement.

I always argued with my father when I wanted to do something that I was afraid would embarrass him, like telling my boss that I had to have an extra week off in August because I was going to college the next month, which wasn't true at all, of course. My father was excruciatingly honest, but I didn't care about his scruples because my business was my business, after all. I think I was practicing for the convent where I would have to obey all the time and I knew I needed some time away from such scrupulousness. My sister couldn't understand how I always "got away" with conning my father into letting me do something she wasn't allowed to do. I think my determination to get my own way made him give in because it was easier than arguing, or maybe it was because he knew he would miss my pushing him to let me do what I wanted after September.

All of the fun of that negotiating evaporated once I entered the convent. The banter disappeared; the back-and-forth of the arguing until a decision was made vanished. Once we were in the convent, only the superiors knew the major facts about anything important in our lives, an evident fact even when it was time for us to go on a vacation. Everything remained vague. Would some of my friends be there on the same week? How would I get there? How long would I be staying? All the fun of planning a vacation had dissipated. I thought longingly of our vacation discussions when I lived at home. Conflict occurred, of course, but our family was a group, unlike the disparity of the conglomeration of people in the convent.

I spent a few hours simmering with anger, as I wondered if my friends would be at our vacation spot at the same time as I would be. *You are lucky*, I reminded myself sternly. *God is giving you a vacation in a beautiful place on Long Island where, with a little more luck, some of your friends might be staying at the same time.*

Most of us dealt that way with the secrecy that pervaded the decisions that were made on our behalf by superiors. At first, we were furious, but then we realized that nothing could be done and we had better keep quiet. We tried to calm ourselves and think of future days when, perhaps, we would be superiors with some kind of power to change the rules that made life so maddening.

With luck, I told myself, two or three of my friends would vacation on the same week, and I would room with them. We would be ecstatic, and run around the place celebrating, giving each other rib-breaking bear hugs when we saw one another. It would be almost as good as if we had planned it ourselves. In the old days, we would have decided that God had planned it, but we were a little older now and did not have the same notion of God as the Master behind everything that happened to us. It used to strain my brain to think that He manipulated everything in my life. Of course, I thought He had a hand in it, but not complete control. If you had told me that the superiors did have complete control, I would have been more inclined to believe that, because that was what I saw all the time. They could change the place where I went for vacation, and the time, and who I would be with. And if I objected, they would make a funny, prissy face and act as if I might have to do a penance soon if I kept on objecting to God's will as determined by them. It all boiled down to letting them have power over me or else I would find out that I had no control at all. As it turned out, they assigned me to a desirable place on Long Island, and I spent several days hoping that some of my friends would be there the same week.

Once I met the Superior of the vacation place, I could go off on my own. I rushed to see the names listed on each room, and found my name, and those of several of my buddies, too, four of us sharing the same accommodations. Our room was huge and, outside our spacious window, we saw the lake and a ring of trees in the distance. Closer to the window was a big well-kept lawn with plastic chairs carelessly left askew by their previous inhabitants. No one seemed to be concerned with keeping everything neat and tidy, unlike most convents. It was relaxing to be away from all the neatness that used to drive me crazy. I felt my mind expand just seeing those chairs, kind of sloppy and misplaced. It made me feel like I was in a normal setting again, like home, where my mother was neat but not ridiculously so. In the convent, I always felt that there was this big banner hanging over my head, reminding me that neatness is next to godliness. Or was it cleanliness? Whatever! They were all things at which I did not excel.

Ann and Betty and Therese were already there in their room, making the beds and grinning at each other as if they had short-sheeted my bed...but they hadn't. They knew I would find a way to get even in some way if they played a trick on me! It was like we were kids again, no rules, no parents who were checking on us all the time, just friends. It was great. I wanted to stay there forever, not just one week, but forever.

The bell for dinner rang and we remembered that we were still in the convent, but it didn't matter because we could talk and swing our arms and scoot up and down the wide staircase, our habits sweeping the stairs, and no one objecting to the clattering of our feet. We hurried into the dining room and suddenly the convent reentered our lives in the person of a harried-looking older woman who announced that we would be assigned seats for meals. God, did it never end, these people bossing us around? I glanced at Therese, who muttered that this woman who had intruded on our joy happened to be the superior of the vacation villa where we were staying.

"Sister-I-am-In-Charge" hustled me over to an empty chair at a table already filled with five or six sisters. One of them began talking to me before I even sat down. She kept on and on, in a loud voice, not making too much sense, and not waiting for a response from me. I suddenly realized that, when you came to this lovely vacation spot, part of your time would be spent eating with mentally ill sisters who were there for a rest cure. Every other seat at the table was taken by a sister who was there for a vacation like I was, and/or by a mentally ill sister who was chattering, not making any sense, or silent and downcast. I could hardly believe my eyes. Of course, I had no one to complain to. I would have to make the best of it. After the first shock, I began to feel sorry for these poor souls who were so lost. Besides, my friends also were here, and when I wasn't at meals, I would be with them, anywhere on the grounds that I chose. But even now, after so many years, the shock of it remains with me, and the disappointment.

The beauty of that Villa was enough to make you want to cry. Originally, it had belonged to a wealthy man who bequeathed it to the Motherhouse to use as they chose. There were porches leading out from most of the rooms and wide windows with filmy curtains that let in light and air to soothe us. Just being there made us happy. We were used to dark little rooms in our convents with linoleum floors and such narrow hallways that only one person at a time could navigate them. We found peace here in the Villa. That same peace probably led earlier superiors to put so many mentally ill sisters here. We could feel ourselves relax away from the poverty-stricken neighborhoods where we worked and the confusion and chaos of our lives. It was a wonderful place for a vacation and I was grateful to be there.

The four of us explored the grounds the second day, including the little sliver of land just outside the entrance into the Villa where the local stores began usurping the quiet of our new home. A dignified hubbub always prevailed at those stores, with their fancy products and the tiny discreet price tags that the storeowners used to emphasize that they were not gauche like so many others in the less desirable parts of town. A wealthy area, it hosted plenty of wealthy girls, shopping with their equally wealthy friends. Once, when we passed an ice-cream store that we dared peek into, we saw an advertisement for cones that added caviar to the peaked towers of ice-cream. Two giggling girls passed us with their cones dripping little bullets of black caviar onto their manicured hands. They acted bored, as if they were used to wasting exotic foods. We hurried back to the Villa where we felt safe, where we knew we belonged.

We ventured outside the boundary lines of the Villa only that one time. Sometimes we hiked around the lake, with its silvery fish gliding just under the surface of the water. We looked at the shadowy trees and tried to remember quotations from poetry books that fit our mood. But that bored us quickly, and none of us could remember more than a few lines anyway. After we stopped trying to be intellectual or religious, we dropped the pretense and hitched up our skirts and tucked them into our belts so we could tramp easily through the thick vegetation. We talked about our friendships and how lucky we were to be together. We never even said a formal prayer.

One evening a sudden thunder storm whipped its way into our peaceful surroundings, just as we were leaving for the lake. "Sister-I-am-In-Charge" appeared out of nowhere, and hissed at us to stay away from our rooms with those wonderful windows. My three pals retreated to the musty library and flopped onto the broken-down lounge chairs. I decided to visit an old sister who was in the last stages of cancer in the Villa infirmary. She still gave a sweet smile to anyone who bothered to stop by her bed. I had not met too many sisters that I wanted to model my life after, but in this gentle soul I found one of them. It made me stop and think that maybe it really could be worth it to stay in the convent until "the last dog was hung," as my mother would say. Maybe I could keep my personality and still love Jesus above anyone else.

When I wandered back to the library, the four of us returned to our discussions of how we could manage to see each other more frequently during the year, and how we could change the rules that were driving us crazy. It all seemed impossible at the time. Maybe it was just a question we were still not ready to answer.

When the vacation ended, we returned to our convents and our lives, but we always remembered the lake at the Villa, the fragile mentally ill who were our dinner companions, the beauty of that lovely place, and the friends that lived with us for that wonderful week. It may not have been a trip to Alaska or to Greece, but it comforted our souls. Like the old saying in the Bible, it poured out on us the balm of Gilead. We needed nothing more.

BOSSING A PRIEST AROUND; A RARE OCCURRENCE INDEED

The only priest I ever had the nerve to boss around was a young man who had recently been assigned to the parish where I had taught for three years. Ordinarily, I was too timid to tell priests "off," as my mother would have described it, but rage is a great leveler when some priest with his head in ecclesiastical clouds needs to come down to earth in a hurry.

Nancy, a bright, loving girl from last year's eighth grade graduating class was dying of leukemia and no one had come to her house even once to hold her hand, smooth her hair, or listen to her teen-age fears. I marched over to the rectory to let the gentle pastor of the church know that one of his suffering parishioners needed someone to visit this fragile young girl before it was too late to say, "I'm sorry," to her mother.

He started to say, "I'll be there tomorrow," but I interrupted him. "Ask Father Gotti to go today and maybe every day. Her mother doesn't think she has too long to live."

He looked startled at my demand. It was almost an order. I usually didn't have the courage to be so direct, but it wasn't me that I was asking for. It was for Nancy.

A lot of the eighth grade girls had teenage crushes on Father Gotti, and Nancy, who was shy, used to position herself at the back of the group of girls who waited for him to come out of the sacristy after Mass. Sometimes, if he was delayed, she slipped away before the other girls left. She looked pale and her mother usually caught up with her and opened the car door so that Nancy could have a ride home, although it was only a few blocks to her house. Her mother looked worn out. She smiled a little when I told her what I had done. "Nancy will be so happy to see him," she said, and patted my arm.

I stopped at the rectory that afternoon to tell Father Gotti that Nancy's mother would be waiting for him at their house. "Please don't let anyone else come. You are the one she needs," I directed him. It was like the big notices on cheap menus that said, "No Substitutions Allowed." Nancy's mother and I were like an army of two, and we both felt stronger after I had assured her that Father Gotti would come.

He visited Nancy that day and told me later how shocked he had been when he saw her, shrunken like an old lady.

"She looks so different," he said. "I don't know how her mother bears it."

I would have been afraid I was doing things wrong, but he barreled ahead, fed her some lifesavers that she promptly vomited up, held her hand while her face was being washed and, according to her mother, didn't flinch at the mess. He was a good lesson in how to handle an awkward moment with the tenderness that Nancy needed so badly. It probably did her more good than any special medicine the hospital could have given her.

The next few days were tough all around. Nancy was moved unexpectedly to the critical care unit in the cancer hospital, and I rushed in to see her. Someone else had given her a poem written by a Civil War soldier that talked about praying for strength and being given weakness instead. There were several other similes in the poem, but it ended, "I was given nothing that I asked for, but I received all things I had hoped for." The poem was glued onto the bed rail where she could read it at will. I wondered who had given it to her. It gave her strength, and I was glad that someone had found it and brought it to her.

I didn't talk religion to her. I felt that she could get all that from Father Gotti, and maybe all she wanted from me, if anything, was a smile, and a gentle pat on her emaciated hand. She knew what was happening to her. I said, "I love you so much, Nancy," each time I left and hoped that was enough.

She died a week later. Father Gotti said the funeral Mass, and her mother walked behind the closed coffin with her arms outstretched in a longing gesture that was louder than any words anyone could have said.

About a month later, her mother called me and asked me if I could come to the house, look at all the sympathy cards that had been sent in memory of Nancy, and have lunch with her. The Superior said I could go to the cemetery and look at the cards there and sit with the mother in her car, but I could not eat with a person who was not a priest or a nun. It was typical of the ridiculous rules that we had been taught in the novitiate. Heaven forbid that I eat with a secular person, as if some barrier would be breached by such a thing. But I was too tied up in all the rigidity of the convent rules. I dared not disobey them, though I was beginning to sense their foolishness. I was afraid of offending God but, even worse, I was scared to death of standing up to the superior. Nancy's mother wanted desperately for me to visit Nancy's room and see the special memorials that had been sent by friends. I had a feeling it would comfort her if I saw them. But I was too bound by my fears.

The Superior finally said I could go to the cemetery, so I went one afternoon and sat near Nancy's grave and sobbed with the mother. We hugged one another, probably in lieu of embracing Nancy. Together, we looked at every one of the cards she had received, and wept over each of them. She gave me an elaborate prayer card from the funeral, with the words, "Bride of Christ" on the front of the card and, on the inside, a little picture of Nancy that looked like her sweet self before the leukemia had struck. I don't think the mother ever understood the significance of the words," Bride of Christ" on that card, but I did. Despite all her youth, and immaturity, Nancy had stripped away the things that masqueraded as love---love for her mother, and even for me. I never forgot her. I have carelessly lost many things since then, but the prayer card and Nancy's memory remain intact.

Finding New Horizons

When the summer ended, I left the ghetto and returned to the old-fashioned convent where I had lived for the past few years. My strong feelings of nostalgia for the friends I made during that summer, while I worked in the ghetto, were mixed with an undeniable sense of relief at seeing it all end. The work was admirable, the living was adventurous, and the companionship of the sisters comforted me. But when I compared myself to some of the truly heroic sisters who had lived in the stark surroundings of barely-livable buildings day after day, I knew I lacked the valor to live forever in that environment. In addition to not wanting to live the rest of my life perpetually looking over my shoulder at every vagrant in the neighborhood, I didn't want to live in a building where the pipes leaked every other week, and dirty water ran down the walls and into the gutters near the doorway to the house. I was honest enough to know that I lacked the inner strength to live in buildings that were falling apart.

Work as the "magazine lady" in the hospital wards was one thing; the thought of daily labor in the dangerous neighborhoods of Brooklyn was quite another. It scared me. A traditional convent with its stereotypical roles no longer appealed to me, although there I found many sisters in those convents to admire and love dearly. Teaching, with its exhausting demands, no longer attracted me. I had recently earned my doctorate in counseling from a well-known university and I was curious to learn if actually using what I had studied would lessen the feelings of discontent that nagged at me.

In quiet moments, when I should have meditated, I sometimes asked myself, *Does part of my boredom come from living with only women day after day?*

The thought of friendships with personable men frightened and exhilarated me at the same time. Living with both genders was not something in which I was interested, although a few celibate mixed-communities could be found here and there. One of my closest friends lived in such a group for a few years, but left it for more independent living. I never asked her why.

The most astounding part of ongoing changes in religious communities was the fact that our Motherhouse had begun allowing us to choose what we wanted to do and where we chose to live. Suddenly, I had the options of staying in my present location, searching out another place to live, and even going on to another form of work. If I received a higher salary by going to a new job, more of my earnings would have to be sent to the Motherhouse to support the sisters who were no longer able to work. I began to feel sorry for Mother Josepha when I remembered her endless classes on the vow of poverty a few years ago.

The whole thing has boiled down to living an independent life as long as the larger community can maintain itself and care for any infirm or elderly sisters, I thought in astonishment one day. What I did not foresee was that sisters who had always depended on the community to provide companionship and a stable way of life might be unhappy with these changes. *The whole concept of community is being individualized slowly but surely. What will it be like in another twenty years?* I thought to myself.

When the Pope belted out, in his strong, full-bodied voice, "Women can now share more fully in the Church's apostolate," I knew that the "old days," when I walked in lock-step and quietly said my rosary, were coming to an end. Priests, who had asserted an authoritarian role over us, knew that their unending control was beginning to slip away. Not all of them were smiling when they realized what was happening, but there was nothing they could do. I almost felt sorry for them. They had cracked the whip at us for years and so had some superiors. Now we were all equal.

Only we, who had been held down for so many years by superiors and clergy alike, could understand the gasping joy of it all, the horizons that were opened to us by that amazing Pope. It was such a splendid opportunity to lead our own lives, try out other areas of work, and test once-controversial arrangements for living. We who had been silent for so long watched, with delighted clarity, as Pope John 23rd's increased respect for both the laity and the religious orders changed our lives. It was a whole new world, and I leapt at the chance to be part of it.

But how soon would I be able to make the change? I still lived in a traditional convent with Sister Olympia, who was a kind superior but one who continued to hold on to many of the old-fashioned regulations with which all of us were familiar. The very idea of my having a choice left me feeling a little unnerved. All these laws had made me feel safe as I followed the rigid regulations of the founders in Germany. Their solemn faces had glared at me from picture after picture on the novitiate walls, silently warning me not to change even an iota of their stifling laws.

If I ever leave the convent, I used to think to myself, *I will probably marry some bluff Irishman and give my life over to him. It's a safe path I'm used to. He can make all the rules, just like in the old days. It seems like a good starting point*, I said jokingly to myself.

I heard of a group of sisters who lived in a poverty-stricken area of Brooklyn and who I hoped had room for one additional member in their small apartment. I knew a member of the group, Miriam, who was the only one who had been trained in the same old-fashioned Motherhouse where I had prayed, done penances, and learned what being a nun meant. The others came from different religious communities, with their own special rules and traditions. It would be like leaving my family all over again.

I need to make this change in my life, I told myself, and nervously sent a brief note to Miriam, hoping she would say they had no room, or it was too late in the school year to expect Sister Olympia to search out a teacher to take my place at the school. But it didn't work out that way at all.

The answer was bittersweet.

"If we had the room," Miriam quickly responded, "you would be welcome."

What good is that? I said to myself. *You don't have the room, so I have to find another place.*

Then Miriam called, "One sister in our group just received a special assignment and is going to be away for a full year. You are very welcome to come here, but when she returns, you will have to find another place to live."

So it was all falling into place. Sister Olympia knew that I had been restless all year, and had hoped that trying something new would help me. I swallowed hard when I got Miriam's answer. Sister Olympia just patted my hand and said I could always come back, if I didn't like it in my new place. She didn't push me either way. She was rather an amazing woman, like a good mother who encouraged her children to follow their own pathways. I knew I would miss her.

I packed up my meager belongings at the convent where I had been living for the past several years, and arranged for a car-ride to my new home. I told the sisters at my old place that I would be coming back in a few months but my fingers were crossed behind my back. I had no idea if I would ever return to a traditional convent.

The cook, especially, was sorry to see me leave, because we had built up a pleasant friendship over the years. Agatha was an old German sister who, at Christmas time, made wonderful cookies which she arranged proudly on big platters. She still had a pronounced German accent. I had a lot of interest in her family, who were all located in Chicago where my sister had lived for several years. Without any money, Agatha never got to see them. I had this daydream that someday Agatha and I would slip off to the airport, fly to Chicago, and surprise her family. We would wildly start knocking on their door, she with a big box of cookies and me with a happy grin.

Part of that dream did come to pass for her when I asked the Superior if I could buy an airline ticket for Agatha out of my meager savings and send her, complete with cookies, to spend a week or so with her family. Agatha was almost in tears when I told her of my grand idea, "The Agatha Adventure," as I privately dubbed it.

This is another adventure, "The Mary Adventure," I told myself as the sisters from my old convent, who had driven me to my new home, pulled up to a nondescript building located in a miserable neighborhood in Brooklyn. Loud music poured out of a noisy bar located on the floor directly below my new home.

I had heard a scary story about those bars that existed on almost every corner in this area. Two sisters from another convent moved into an apartment with the naïve but laudable purpose of trying to establish what we called "a presence" in the neighborhood. The two of them decided to go to a local bar in order to let the customers there see that they were "ordinary folk" who wanted to share in the lives of others. It made sense to me, when I was in the novitiate, to take every chance I could to slip in a word about God. Now, that whole concept began to sound, "a bit over the top" as my sister would say.

Well, I muttered to myself, *I'd better ask Miriam if she knows the end of that story, before I move into a small group to live. What kind of chances are nuns willing to take?*

When Miriam told me the rest of the story, I shuddered.

"A scruffy man in the bar grabbed hold of one of the nuns and wouldn't let her go," Miriam began. "He began dancing with his body pressed hard against her. No one tried to interfere, not even her companion who stood, white-faced, staring at them."

"Didn't anyone say anything?" I questioned.

Miriam just looked at me as if I had a lot to learn. "No," she said. "He just began to whisper something in his unwilling dance-partner's ear."

We heard later from her companion that it was a warning to her, a warning laden with words that she only had seen scrawled on the door of an abandoned building near her apartment. She was foolish, terribly foolish, and this man was wise in the ways of the world of bars and drunken men. He wanted to frighten her before something happened to her that would be far worse than a little close dancing.

One of the other men in the bar shouted after them, as her dance-partner shoved her and the other sister out the barroom door. "You don't belong here. If you know what's good for you, you won't come into a bar again."

It was a strange way of being protective, but maybe no other lesson would have gotten through to them. The story was one that remained with me. We always would have to be careful in areas where we were not wearing our habits, if we were foolish enough to wander into places where we shouldn't be.

The sisters who drove me there couldn't leave their car to help me with my possessions, for fear the car would vanish.

I wish someone were here to lend me a helping hand, I thought, as I lugged my suitcase up the broken cement steps to ring the doorbell. A few neighborhood kids who had sprawled on the steps moved grudgingly aside to make room for me while I waited anxiously for someone to appear. Finally, a tall, thin sister opened the door with a broad smile and took my suitcase.

"Hi! I'm Ellen," she said. "Watch the stairs. They're a little wobbly."

I grabbed for the banister, just in case.

The apartment was on the second floor. Actually, it was what they used to call a "railroad flat," because the bedrooms were located along both sides of a long hallway. Ellen deposited my suitcase in a small room with an old dresser, a little lamp that gave off a feeble light, and a firm-looking bed that someone had managed to squeeze into the space nearest to the door. Near my room, in a large kitchen, a teakettle whistled a welcome. A Formica-topped table with a handwritten name tag designated me as the "new gal on the block," which made me smile. Pat, one of the sisters, warned me that they had a "little problem" with cockroaches, but had checked all the pots and pans, and even the teakettle, before I came. She had a twinkle in her eye, but I had an uneasy feeling she wasn't kidding.

The dinner was festive. *Someone here is a good cook*, I reflected as I dug into some fried chicken and baked potatoes. I began to relax a bit, although I desperately wanted to ask them if roaches were able to scamper up the bedclothes and get into the beds with us. As the four of us continued to eat, we talked about the neighborhood, what work the sisters did, and what their lives were like here in the slums. We talked about Pope John the 23rd and the changes the rotund little man had made in our church when he threw open the windows and said, "Let the fresh air in."

We were in the front lines now ourselves, but we hardly knew it. We wanted only to live our lives more independently, have a bit of the money that we made, and still be nuns. We asked for little and too often were made by frightened superiors to feel that it was too much. But we kept on suggesting new obstacles for the next brave crusaders to attack. I thought our revolutionary pope would cheer us on in our quest for freedom. At least, I hoped he would.

The next morning, we talked in greater detail about the type of work each of us did. Miriam, a close friend from earlier days, taught in a nearby school and seemed to be quite satisfied with her work. Pat, the cockroach killer, was a kind of informal social worker, warm and friendly, with a smile that drew people in. Ellen, a part-time hospital worker, was tall and slender, rather serious-looking, and quiet. And then there was me, eager and excited, happy to be living in an adventure, and sharing it with sisters who did not seem as bound by the rigidity of a million rules, but still and all, were lovers of God.

My own job was as a psychologist with a small branch of Catholic Charities, located in a seedy area a few blocks away from an evil-looking bridge near the Expressway, where vagrants tried to sleep at night. Later, a priest was murdered under that bridge, his body naked and his empty wallet tossed a few feet away. We heard rumors that he was homosexual and had been stabbed when he refused to pay the partner for a few moments of pleasure. It was one of those scandals that faded after a few days, but the ugliness of it stayed with me. I never had known any homosexual priests. I kept wishing that someone would come forward and prove that he was being falsely accused. Homosexuality among priests was not talked about among nuns at that time, and the rumors gradually faded. I worked in the Catholic Charities building in the daytime, and felt safe. I wondered if Betty, my old friend from my days with Sister Waltruda, knew about such things. We still were blessedly innocent.

I worked as a team with an Irish priest, Father Doherty, who as yet did not have his doctorate. I was more qualified, on paper at least, than he was, a fact that came back to haunt me later on. Each of us was paid on the same salary line, which to me was a fortune. The two of us never discussed money. It seemed unimportant, because the purse strings were held tightly by the bishop and any change in reimbursement was unlikely.

Father Doherty was about my own age, and eager to begin his ministry in this godforsaken area of humanity. He lived with a few other priests in a nearby location and knew that I had recently moved in with some other sisters. His mild interest in my life matched the bored attention I had received from other parish priests. The only difference was his vague surprise that I already had my doctorate.

I imagined him saying, "Why did you bother to get an advanced degree? You'll probably get tired of this little adventure and scurry back to teaching."

He still struggled with his dissertation and hoped to complete it within the next few years. When I tried to describe him to my friends, I called him an empty shell, non-threatening but dull. He probably felt the same way about me. No emotional excitement boiled between us, which probably was just as well.

I had already heard rumors about priests getting involved with nuns here and there, now that there was more freedom in our comings and goings. The thought made me question what I would do if an attractive priest approached me. *Do I want that for myself?* I quietly thought when I could sit and meditate on life's choices.

I floundered as I tried to find my way in a new job, especially in these surroundings that were infinitely different from life in the traditional convent. I decided to concentrate on my counseling assignments and figure out the best way to make a go of it with Father Doherty as my co-worker. Love affairs with priests were not high on my agenda, and getting used to Father Doherty, who I already had seen could be rather caustic, would be enough for me to handle if I were to succeed as a counselor.

I looked around at the clients who were already ambling into the center as soon as the doors opened. They were looking for help, asking questions about food stamps, and generally acting nervous at the sudden change in staff from black to white. Among them were a mix of poor black people who lived in the area and a smattering of Caucasian women who had somehow heard of the center and were searching for answers. Many of the poorest people went directly to the ministers in the storefront churches, or they turned to their own families, who had dealt with similar problems and were eager to give them "home-grown" solutions. I supposed the fact that neither Father Doherty nor I were black probably made them view our solutions as somewhat biased. We were eager to help them but, because they consulted us on an "as needed basis," we never had a chance to build up a real relationship with anyone. I was too involved in myself to want to reach out to a wide group of new people at that time anyway. In the end, I realized that, as long as they felt comfortable with me, maybe I could help them, and that was all that I wanted.

As long as we had clients coming in daily, Father Doherty didn't mutter any complaints. He was, in my opinion, "a cold fish," but a decent diagnostician. As long as we discussed the psychological problems of our clients, we maintained a useful relationship. As for me, I didn't mind having a breather from the poor souls that I had met in the local hospital the summer before when I was a "magazine lady," dispensing glossy out-of-date tomes to dreadfully sick patients in their rumpled beds. I cared about those people in their misery, but knew I was only a passing presence in their lives. In the same way, I cared about our ghetto clients. I saw clearly that their problems required more expertise than either of us had.

So we met our daily clientele. We gave them procedures for dealing with the vagaries of the Welfare offices, or the Food Stamp program that was doling out huge packages of cheese or recipes for peanut-butter soup. We saw weary-looking mothers who brought sullen pregnant daughters to our office for advice on how to find the prospective fathers, who disappeared as soon as the unwelcome news was delivered to them. There was never any talk of marriage, not even from the girls' mothers, who knew only too well that marriage to the babies' fathers was unlikely to result in any money. These all were problems that had no answers, not in our clinic nor in any storefront church either.

Father Doherty and I decided to bring in a local public health nurse to give talks on birth control. Secretly, I viewed this innovation as an idea doomed to failure, but I encouraged him to proceed with requesting the needed funds anyway, just in case it became a success. Other than providing a few giggles for our little group of teenagers, it did nothing to help the "situation," as we referred privately to the caseload of angry pregnant girls who were forced to see us by their exasperated mothers.

There was such chaos in the families that we, who wanted to help people, didn't believe information on sexual behavior would really help. The mothers could have given the course themselves. For the daughters, who had already experimented in that arena, it was "too little, too late." Despite our best efforts, we were so awkward when the subject came up that the girls knew they should avoid it. So they did. Instead, we tried to move on to job training and school behavior, about which I, at least, knew practical approaches. The whole thing seemed hopeless to me. Maybe I should go back to teaching little kids how to spell or to arithmetic problems, where I at least didn't blush when I discussed the lesson for the day.

I couldn't speak for Father Doherty's knowledge in the areas of sex, but mine was confined to the few classes I had in the novitiate before taking my vow of chastity. It had been a time of blushing and quiet reading of a few pages on the subject that Mother Josepha, who didn't know much more than we did, had provided. At least I had dated before I entered the convent, so I could claim a little knowledge, mostly gained by whispering with my girlfriends when a few of the "wilder girls" came into our high school class with hickeys on their necks. I had no idea how comfortable Father Doherty was in any of these areas. We were like "babes in the woods," stumbling along in a world awash in promiscuity, where people yelled out curses to one another, or wrote rude words on the walls of empty buildings. Most of our efforts were doomed to failure and we were savvy enough to know that. We tried to concentrate on what we called our more "normal" clients, who were themselves lost in a fog of confusion about their own lives but at least had problems with possible solutions that could be found in magazines like "Psychology Today," or in a questionnaire in "Cosmopolitan." We didn't have much success with those, either.

There was only one case of family counseling that we both always remembered, not because we were successful, but because there were 25 people in the family, who arrived as a unit. They babbled constantly, each one trying to get their chance to make their point with us, the counselors, who they obviously regarded as their father or mother figure. Father Doherty and I used to make charts that would group the more talkative members of the family in one corner of the room, and the better-behaved members in another corner. Then we directed them to the proper section as they gained more control over their verbal interactions with the other family members. Nothing worked, and the Tower of Babel continued to reign. What a colossal failure in the annals of counseling, but it made a hilarious story for anyone who would listen when we were asked how our day went. At least we tried!

I was beginning to think that doing so-called counseling with people whose lives were already ruined was not going to be fulfilling regardless of the ethnic or social level of the clients. They had long ago passed the line of succeeding in life, and I knew it. I wasn't sure if Father Doherty had faced it yet, and it was not my place to tell him. Working with him was necessary so I could pay my rent at the apartment and send money to the Motherhouse. We both labored at our fruitless jobs, and hoped that at least one of our clients would one day figure out an answer to their problems with or without our help. I was counting the days until we got paid. At least I would have something tangible in my hands to prove to myself that I had really been working all these days.

When the first payday finally came, I rushed to the nearest bank to open a checking account. I was ecstatic. It was the first time in nine years that I would have my own money.

Why is that so exciting to me? Didn't I make a vow of poverty ten years ago? I mused as I looked forward to my first payday. I felt guilty as I wondered how much dedication I really had to my vows. Something in me was definitely changing. I wasn't mercenary, but I kept remembering that I was being paid because of my work, not because the Bishop was feeling charitable. So didn't I have every right to expect some of that money to stay in my pocket? And Father Doherty, my compatriot at Catholic Charities, had mentioned last week that we were each being paid close to $150 for two weeks work.

Just thinking about that money made me feel rich. Rich, at least until the bank manager informed me that I could not cash that precious check, nor any others that Catholic Charities gave me, as long as the black letters, IN TRUST were printed after my own name.

"That means," he explained carefully, as if I were in kindergarten, "that the money will be paid to the convent, not to you."

What! I said to myself. *Paid to the convent? I'll be lucky if I see a dollar of it.*

I couldn't believe what I had just heard. I wanted to yell or run weeping out of the bank but I just sat there clinging to the edge of the chair, as if maybe staying in the bank would change things for me. The manager kept waiting for me to move, tapping his fingers on the hardwood desk, but I had no place to go.

What is the use of working, I thought, *if I never get any money?*

I had had no idea that I would have to hand my whole salary over to the convent. What would I be getting out of working, if I couldn't keep even a few dollars for my own pleasure?

Money means something to you, Mary, I finally acknowledged to myself in shocked amazement. *In fact, it means a lot!*

For some reason, my banker, as I had begun to think of him, suddenly said to wait a minute. He hurried over to another office, spoke to a bored-looking man, and came back with a confused but happy expression on his face.

"Mr. Clifton, the Bank Manager, found a loophole," he declared with a toothy smile and handed me a sheaf of documents. "These papers will give you the right to open a bank account in your own name, sign personal checks, and even add up your balance if you ever want to."

I felt like kissing him on both cheeks like they do in the French movies. I felt like dancing with him up and down the aisles where the solemn-looking bank managers filled out stacks of forms on their cluttered desks. I felt like falling on my knees right in the bank, and looking up to the heavens, and yelling, "Thank you, Jesus!" I felt like crying with joy.

At last I had money under my own control. I didn't care if I never got another raise. For the first time in oh-so-many years, I had money of my own. It was what they called in all the Nancy Drew stories, a "red-letter day." The exuberance of that day stayed with me for weeks.

Unfortunately, my delight was tempered by the fact that money which had usually been decreed in Church sermons as the "root of all evils," was also not the cure for all ills. Life in a group of four sisters was a little harder that I had anticipated. There was no place to go to in that tiny apartment when you needed to "get away" for a few hours. Taking a walk was out of the question, unless you wanted to hear someone yell out "Honky" as you passed, or to be a target of some kid's spitball as you neared his apartment window. I could feel tensions build up that I had not anticipated, even though I was pleased that I had made the change. Now that I had money of my own, I decided to go for therapy to Rose, an untrained therapist that my friend Miriam had gone to for the past few years.

THERAPY, WHERE HAVE YOU BEEN ALL MY LIFE!

Rose saw her clients in her tiny apartment, which was adjacent to Bloomingdale's fancy department store. What a coup! If I went a few minutes early, I could wander in and out of Bloomingdale's with all the wealthy ladies, getting doused with expensive perfume. My weekly exercise consisted of struggling up and down the winding stairs to reach Rose's second floor apartment, hanging on for dear life to the shaky banisters.

Once I arrived inside the door, I found myself in the midst of all kinds of wonderful artwork. Rose was an accomplished artist and had traveled all over the world. Even her little bathroom was jammed with funny-looking naked figurines engaged in mysterious contortions. I wondered what they were doing with one another. I wanted to ask Rose, but I felt uncomfortable questioning her. I thought it might be one question too many. It was an adventure just to be there, with this wild-haired woman who looked like a displaced gypsy.

After several weeks, as a special treat, Rose took me for a few sessions to her sculpture studio, located on the third floor overlooking the old Klein's Department store in Union Square. When I peered out the dirty windows, I watched people elbowing each other, eager to reach different departments so they could snatch the best bargains in men's shirts, women's underwear, cheap jewelry, and any other items for which New Yorkers might hanker.

Sometimes, I wandered among Rose's statues, looking out of the corner of my eye at the massive Biblical figures standing at attention. Moses, Abraham, and Isaac were there in their bold splendor, listening to my problems. Her sculptures, with their blatant nakedness, embarrassed me. Once or twice, a secret part of me rejoiced at being in such a decadent atmosphere, I who had seen only decorous statues in my convent chapels. I made believe that I thought her sculptures were prize-worthy. It was the least I could do for this wonderful woman, who had many of her own quirks, yet still had time for mine. My lessons in male anatomy were sneakily pursued but never discussed with Rose. I preferred to blush in private. Exploring my sexual fantasies had not yet entered my world of therapy.

After a few months, once we had thoroughly discussed mine, she told me about her own troubles. A priest who was a friend of hers wanted to have sex with her, to find out what it was like. I was horrified at his selfishness. After this one event, he never called her again. There was no more sex and no more friendship. This was quite a lesson for me. I watched Rose mourn his absence deeply and I mourned with her. She used her own lapse of good sense as a warning to me, to be careful in any relationships I might have in the future.

"Men can be very selfish," she said to me, and I knew she was talking about my lurking future as well as her betrayal by this priest. I didn't plan on looking for any sex in my life yet, but Rose was aware, without my talking about it, that the time would come when I would attach myself to some man. I would need to remember the lessons from her life if I were to untangle myself from someone who was too selfish to love me. She knew, too, that I would probably not involve myself with a man until I decided to leave the convent. That was a step that I did not yet contemplate.

Once in a while, I thought how amazing it was that I, who entered the convent when I was only eighteen years old, and had only one timid guy in high school as a boyfriend, was now being told the troubles of my therapist. It was strange, but even stranger was the fact that it didn't bother me, or lessen my faith in her. So I stayed with her, her quirky art work, and her massive sculptures for two years before I moved on to a more classical therapist. The physician's oath decrees, "Do no harm!" and Rose, in her open way, had brought me only good things.

Her wild side keyed into my own as yet unexplored personality. Rose wanted me to be more adventurous and decided that I should go on vacation with her one summer. I wasn't so sure that I wanted to.

Maybe she is a lesbian, I thought uncomfortably, but I finally agreed. Off we went on a Greyhound bus to a little town in upstate New York where we scurried off to a boarding house that had a few rooms for rent. The rooms were ordinary, but the surroundings were lovely. There were no religious rules to observe or chapel where I had to pray, which was a relief to me. God was part of my life, but in a very informal way. Besides, I had decided that whatever Rose was, she was not a lesbian.

Each day we packed a lunch and wandered around the area, talking and laughing and quietly making fun of people who were what we considered "hicks," as if we were sophisticated. I certainly wasn't, and she, in some ways, was still a kid. I even felt a little guilty making fun of them, although they couldn't hear us.

One evening we passed an old cemetery and she suggested in her bossy way, "Let's go in and sit on some of the flat grave stones."

I was shocked. *It shouldn't be so bad,* I told myself suddenly. *It might be fun.*

So there we sat, irreverent as we pleased, sitting and laughing and drinking gin from a small jug she had brought with her. I never had tasted gin in my life, but it was her favorite after-dinner "libation" as she called it. I felt so grown-up drinking and giggling.

Once, we passed a huge old house with a few rocking chairs scattered on its spacious porch. There were no lights on, and Rose decreed in her dictatorial way that no one was home and we could go and sit in their rocking chairs. Up we went and ran to the chairs. For a few moments all was serene. The booming voice of the owner of the house suddenly scared us out of the chairs and down the slope and over the distant gravestones, until we could hear that voice no longer.

I resented Rose in a way for leading me into such strange byways. At the same time, it was such fun to be bold, like a bad little kid. She was always saying to me, "What are you afraid of? You make people into these bug-a-boos. They are nothing. Do what you want."

She was such a mix of emotions. Another day, as we walked along the road, we came to a house where Rose abruptly decided she was thirsty and needed some water. A wasted-looking old man was sitting on his front porch with a mangy dog.

He called out in his raspy voice, "Jane, bring out some water for the nice ladies who just stopped here a minute ago." Rose plopped down on the grass a few yards away from him, her skirt pulled up just past her knees, her legs splayed. I gulped.

A skinny woman with her hair in a loose top-knot, came to the door, saw Rose and shrieked, "Get out, you slut."

Rose laughed triumphantly, and yelled to me, "Come on, Mary."

The man was still grinning, moving back and forth in his chair, as we ran out of the yard. I couldn't dare ask Rose why she sat like that, so carelessly sexy in front of the old man. I didn't understand her. Sometimes, I loved her. Other times, she humiliated me by her conduct. But she was always helping me not to be so afraid of people, whether they were selfish priests who wanted to have sex and leave as soon as it was over or tetchy old wives who probably hadn't let their husbands near them in years.

I decided not to tell Rose about the fat, teenage boy who sat an aisle away from me on the Greyhound bus the day our vacation ended. A woman in her fifties, who wore a lot of lipstick and brightrouge on her cheeks, rubbed her hand up and down on his crotch until he pressed himself into her hand harder and harder and grinned more and more.

I don't have to tell Rose everything, I told myself. *Some things can belong just to me.*

I desperately wanted to see what was going on, only a few bus seats away from me. I wanted to jump up as if I had dropped a magazine and get a glimpse of this exciting behavior before it ended as somehow I knew it must. But I was too slow. It was over. I was annoyed with myself. I had missed my chance, and it might never come again, at least not on this bus. As comfortable as I was with Rose, somehow this was not something I could manage to ask her about. I was still too shy to ask too many questions. I gazed out the window. I wanted to ask Rose about many things, but not today. Maybe not ever.

I still sorely needed her lessons. Maybe a traditional therapist would not have told me to drink gin sitting on a tombstone, or contemplate relaxing on some stranger's porch in their rocking chairs. But then, again, a therapist's words alone might not have pushed me into the wide, open spaces where Rose's bossy behavior, and her engaging artistic wildness had shoved me. Eventually I moved on to a classical therapist, but I never forgot Rose with her bold ways, her gruff voice, and her reliable caring that reminded me always that I was a human being with rights and should not be afraid.

WANTED: A NEW JOB, A NEW PLACE TO LIVE, BUT WHERE?

Toward the end of the school year, the sister who had been on a special assignment for the past year was scheduled to return to our tiny Brooklyn apartment to claim her old room. I had cheerfully agreed when Miriam told me last year that I would have to move at the year's end, but now I felt stunned as if the whole arrangement had been a hoax. I felt adrift once more, as I began looking for a place to settle. Suddenly, I decided not to return to the traditional convent where I had lived for a number of years. The sisters at that site were willing to accept me again but I had tasted independence, and had rejoiced in the thrill of spending my skimpy salary.

It hasn't increased by even a penny, I reminded myself. But it was still my salary and I was strangely satisfied. Father Doherty dropped a hint one day that he had heard a rumor, through his clerical friends, that Catholic Charities intended to shrink the staff at the end of June. He omitted the news that he had already secretly asked one of the administrators to make his position permanent.

I was furious when one of the secretaries whispered this piece of office gossip to me when I slipped into her cubicle one morning. I had more educational credentials and he still worked on his dissertation. It was the first time that I had to face the fact that a man probably had more advantages in the work-place.

The priests in the parishes where I had taught in the crowded schools were the masters over what we did, but I was accustomed to that arrangement and accepted it as part of the package. But this was different. I actually worked in a clinic. Father Doherty and I shared a prim-faced secretary who compulsively re-arranged the chairs in the cramped waiting room where nervous people sat and waited for someone to say, "The counselor will see you now." An edgy, overweight housewife rose and tried to balance her torn shopping bags from the local grocery store, as she herded her four children ahead of her so that I could meet all of them, because no one wanted to be left behind. It was chaotic, but it was a real job in a real clinic. The problem was that what I thought would be an orderly job was just as mixed up as my old classrooms with too many kids all of whom waited for the magic word from the teacher. That, of course, was me, who had no magic words at all.

As I suspected, the permanent position at the clinic went to the wily Father Doherty. All my ranting to the administration at Catholic Charities didn't change that situation. They didn't even have the decency to call me in and give me some fabricated reason why he got the job and I didn't.

"He's no better than I am," I whimpered to a few of my friends.

"But you can always go back to teaching in the schools," they reminded me, and of course they were right.

But it was still unfair.

* * * * *

I tried to remember the words of Pope John the 23rd, about women now sharing more fully in the Church's apostolate and the clergy not being fully effective without them. I was so angry that I couldn't recall a word of that beautiful egalitarian writing. The "little weasel," which was my private name for Father Doherty, was "the man," publicly ordained to do God's work, "a priest forever." I also privately called him "the stealer," someone who connived to grab other people's livelihood. In the end, no matter how many names I called him in private it didn't change the fact that he still had the job. Gradually, in my mind he became the special one and I faded to unworthiness. All of my old feelings of inferiority flooded back. One of my friends, on the brink of saying her marriage vows, told me she had unexpectedly thought as she stood before the altar, "If I couldn't keep my vows to Jesus, can I keep them to my husband?" I had been carefully building up my self-confidence, but Catholic Charities' choice of Father Doherty was undoing it.

Despite my upset feelings, I was just vindictive enough to stay for a few more months so I could get a little more money out of the diocese, by finishing out the remainder of my contract. I wrote a long letter to the administrators at Catholic Charities, and sent a copy to the Bishop. I wasn't used to wildly protesting to superiors when I thought I had been treated unjustly, but my letter made me feel vindicated in some strange way. At least they knew how I felt.

The administrators gave me embarrassed smiles when they ran into me. They never answered the questions that I brought up to them in my letter. The Bishop never responded to me, either. Maybe he was insulted because I had specifically quoted the words of Pope John the 23rd to him about an apostolate being lacking if a woman was not a part of it. That was such a new thought to me. I blushed as I considered it.

Who do you think you are, Mary? I said shyly to myself, as I included that section of the Pope's encyclical in my letter to the Bishop. Maybe His Eminence, as I sarcastically addressed the bishop, had skipped over that sentence when he read the latest essay from the Pope.

Did the Bishop think I was a nun who didn't "know my place" and would have been better off in the classroom where I couldn't do any harm? Did the administrators at Catholic Charities see me as a woman pushing my way into a man's world, where I didn't belong? It was an important lesson for me to learn.

"Watch your back, even if you are a nun. Most people are not out to take advantage of you, but there is always the exception. Be kind, be fair, but take care of yourself." It was not a lesson they taught us in the novitiate, but it was one that would have helped me deal with life, more than their unending lectures on obedience to authority.

You aren't a subservient nun any longer, I said to myself.

There was a song being sung loudly everywhere on the radio, proclaiming, "I am woman, hear me roar," most of which I didn't understand, but which somehow I knew was related to me. It made me feel good, in an odd sort of way.

Now, I not only had to find another job, I had to find another place to live, unless I wanted to go back to teaching and living in a traditional convent. I decided to apply for a job with the New York City Board of Education as a guidance counselor, and rent an apartment where I could live by myself. The position with the Board of Education would be a priceless learning experience. The change in salary would far surpass my formerly proud income from Catholic Charities. A vengeful part of me longed for Father Doherty to know all this. Was this God's way of taking care of me? I actually preferred thinking that I was learning to take care of myself, with Him looking over my shoulder and grinning in God-like approval.

I knew the superiors at the Motherhouse did not care where I worked, but being the first sister in my religious order to live alone in my own apartment was too threatening by far to their traditional way of life. I had to proceed quickly, in order to be sure of a job, as well as an apartment. There was no time to try to persuade them. So I plunged ahead, signed the contract at the Board of Education and rented a basement apartment in Queens, where the ever-faithful Miriam knew the owners. My final action was to send my new address to the Motherhouse, letting them know where I lived. It was my greatest adventure. It involved standing up to the superiors even though I felt awkward and distraught doing so.

They will never understand, I told myself. And I was right.

To Kneel or Not to Kneel — That is My Question

The old monastic custom of kneeling to ask permission to do the simplest things was ingrained in me from novitiate days. When the Council finally made the kneeling rule optional for all of us, I felt a little unnerved. Did that mean that I could choose when I had to kneel? When I followed the rigid regulations of the founders in Germany, all these laws made me feel safe. The solemn faces of the founders glared at me from picture after picture on the novitiate walls. They silently warned me not to change even an iota of their stifling laws.

The first challenge to the new rule came a few weeks later in the form of an invitation sent, not to my superior, but only to me. I gloried in the knowledge that Mother Olympia, lovely as she was when she first took over for Sister Waltruda, no longer was allowed to open my mail. Claire often said that, when power was taken away from the superiors, some of them would struggle with their loss of control. Would Olympia be one of the ones who secretly felt upset when their power was diminished? I wondered if she had held my letter up to the light before she handed my mail to me to see if she could decipher any part of the message inside the thick envelope marked with the return address of the Bishop of our diocese. I grinned at Olympia and stuffed the envelope in my school bag. I felt her eyes follow me as I left the community room.

When I reached my room, I ripped open the envelope and read the embossed invitation inside. Amazement mingled with fear flooded me. The Bishop's office that handled special affairs had sent me an invitation to a fancy dinner in honor of His Eminence, Bishop Heffernan. I was scared to death to accept. I would have to tell the Superior that my invitation to this elegant party came at the request of the parents of a boy whom I had helped resolve some problems. I doubted that Olympia had been invited. Would she have to stay home with the rest of the sisters and eat yesterday's left-over beans while I dined sumptuously without her? The thought of Olympia fuming in the convent dining room, while I was being treated as a celebrity of sorts, was sweet revenge for all the dull meals I had eaten in so much of my convent life, while other superiors occasionally ate at the homes of benefactors of the school. The world was turning upside down and many of us who benefitted from the changes felt confused.

I sat cross-legged on my rumpled bed and thought about the menu. There would be three or four kinds of wine; there would be steak, juicy and dripping with butter; there would be asparagus and mashed potatoes without the lumps that I hated; there would be real ice cream, not the kind that the convent cook made in ice-cube trays, that always had sharp slivers of ice here and there; and at the end of the meal there would be a champagne toast. The napkins would be linen because, after all, he was the Bishop. I would wear my best habit, the only one that had no patches. I would be sitting with the prestigious parents, and smiling at the youngster who had made sure that I was invited. He would be beaming. The Superior would not be there; like Cinderella she had to stay home. When I was transported back to the convent in the parents' Mercedes, I would peek out the tinted windows and wish the trip could be longer. I wanted to savor it a few minutes longer.

Suddenly in the midst of that daydream, I remembered that miserable kneeling regulation. The thought of telling Olympia about my wonderful invitation, and not getting on my knee to ask her permission to attend it, abruptly dissolved my nervous courage. Would she be angry when I asked to go to the dinner with the Bishop? Would she expect to see me on my knee, looking up at her as if she were some kind of a benign goddess, waiting for her consent? Would she silently hope she still had the whip hand over me? I had a choice. Did she depend on my scared little self to kneel?

I jumped off my bed and began to practice that night, over and over, standing ramrod straight, smiling and saying, "Sister Olympia, I am going to the Bishop's dinner on Thursday night. No, I don't need anyone to drive me, because the family will call for me in their Mercedes. I'm sorry you are not going."

That last sentence has to be left out, Mary, I scolded myself. I wanted so much to relieve my own anxiety by adding that insincere sentiment. It was a close call. *You're not sorry, Mary. You're glad!* By the end of my rehearsal, I was almost shouting my little speech. I wasn't sorry at all. I was glad she would be at home eating left-over baked beans and swallowing ice cream with sharp ice slivers in it. I said my speech again and again until my heart stopped pounding. It wasn't that I suddenly started to dislike Sister Olympia. It was just that so many roles had been reversed in our formerly placid convent life and I wasn't sure how those reversals would be received. There was a snippet of revenge stirring in me that had nothing to do with Olympia. It had to do with my growing up and finally having a bit of power in my own life.

The next day, I went to Olympia. Blushing wildly, I stood before her. I looked directly at her emotionless face. I rushed through my carefully rehearsed speech. Her eyes narrowed, and her face turned an ugly red. She said nothing.

I went to the dinner. I laughed at jokes, and I smiled at my hosts. I kissed the cheek of the boy whose parents sent me the invitation. I accepted the ride home in the Mercedes, with its telephone and its tinted windows. I wished the drive were longer, so I could savor it a few more minutes.

Olympia was in her room when I got home. There was a glimmer of light showing through her half-open door. I walked past her room quietly. Her door slammed shut with a reverberating bang. Did she hope I would stop and tell her made up lies that I felt awkward and the parents told me they were sorry they hadn't invited her too? I told her nothing about my wonderful evening. She didn't deserve it.

She never even told me to have a good time. When I reached my own room, I laughed out loud. I couldn't sleep for hours. I reveled in the delights of my beautiful evening of fun and drinks and great food, and of having a few of my humorous comments chuckled over. I knew suddenly that my days of kneeling to speak to another human being were over. What that meant for my future, I didn't know and, much to my astonishment, I didn't care. Not caring was the best part of all! I was preparing myself for a freer life.

Mary Zenchoff

LIVING ALONE AND LOVING IT

Finding a place to live was easy; getting a job was not hard either. Those two steps did not seem difficult to me. The tricky part was to figure out how to get the Motherhouse to agree. Would they want me to go back to the convent where I had been living before I moved to my little hole-in-the-wall in the wilds of Brooklyn? I had had an exciting taste of organizing my own life and didn't want to return to the regulations of the old-style convent. I was too old to put myself in a position where someone else had the right to boss me around. I realized one day, in a sudden flash of fearful amazement, that I didn't even want to bunk in with another group of sisters, no matter how compatible we were. I was like a kid who had been going to college and living in a dorm. The newness and the wonder of it had worn off a long time ago. Now I wanted to go to the next stage in my life. I decided the best thing for me was to find a little apartment, somewhere where I could live alone and have my freedom for a while. After that I would decide what to do with my life. The only thing I was very sure of was that I would still be a nun, somehow or other.

I kept on putting off calling the Motherhouse to tell them that I planned to move and to work for the Board of Education as soon as I could get the financial details worked out. They would be angry, but I knew they didn't want people to leave the convent and would be patient with my decision making.

You're not leaving the convent, I kept telling myself. *You're only adjusting part of it so it will be more to your liking. It's like the old days when you bought a new dress. If the hem wasn't quite right, you brought it to the tailor and watched him fool around with pins sticking out of his mouth every which way, until he had it just right. When he finished, it was still the same material, but it had some of your own style.*

People had fooled around with religious rules for quite a while, especially since Pope John 23rd was elected. The more time I spent in the convent, the more I wanted to be consulted about the changes and be sure that they felt right to me. Superiors had a way of making you feel guilty if you wanted to be part of the process of change, and that niggling guilt still bothered me sometimes.

The part I truly dreaded was trying to persuade Mother Josepha, who was the head of the Motherhouse Council, to let me live alone in my own apartment. Before I could persuade her, I had to convince myself not to be afraid of the power she still had, even now, to control my life. I kept reminding myself that the long days of my childhood were over. They had lasted from the first day I entered the convent when I was 18 years old until now, when I had reached the magic age of 35.

I don't want to live with another group of sisters, no matter how much I love them, I told myself. *The newness and the wonder of that life wore off a while ago. I want to break into the next stage of my life, live alone, be free from bossy superiors for a while. But I still want to be a nun, somehow or other. Is that too much to ask? I want my new life style but still to be called, "Sister Mary." If only Mother Josepha wasn't in charge of my future, maybe I would have a chance.*

I tried to talk to a priest once or twice about the changes I contemplated. I thought he had an intellectual, as well as a spiritual view of religious life, a freer approach. But he acted nervous, as though I was planning to have an affair with him, and abruptly cut off any contact with me.

I'm not looking for an affair with you, I thought angrily. *What a self-centered twerp you are!* I was furious. Being rejected so completely for wanting to grow up a little was a punishment I didn't deserve. I muddled on, talking to my friends. They were more open to change and self-knowledge than any priest had ever been. They had lived the same frustrating life that I had. They understood.

So I put off the call to Mother Josepha as long as I could. I was afraid that in the end I would give in to whatever Mother Josepha thought I should do, the way I had for so many years.

This time, I have to be brave, I told myself. Early one morning, I gritted my teeth, and called Mother Josepha and told her.

* * * * *

One of my dearest friends entered a strict cloistered order when she was 18 years old, and told me once that, when a new set of rules was proclaimed, in order to be sure of pleasing God she decided to destroy all the pictures of her friends as an act of sacrifice. I was horrified.

I wanted to say, "Oh, Eileen, I hope you kept a picture of us when we were silly young things in high school." But I knew she hadn't.

She has Alzheimer's now, and the nun who takes care of her told me that Eileen smiles when she hears my name, but I really don't know if she remembers me. I began to see more and more clearly that the problem with change is often in going too far, sometimes, or maybe not going far enough. It is a delicate balance.

The Buddhists have a saying that, when you are ready for something, a clearer pathway to the change will appear. As I struggled to figure out where I would live if I didn't return to my old room in the local convent where I had lived before moving, to the ghetto apartment, one of my friends who heard of my dilemma. She told me about a couple who were looking for a tenant for their basement apartment. They lived in Queens, in a Mafia neighborhood where John Gotti reigned supreme, and my friends knew I would be safe there. Miriam, my friend from the apartment in the slums, directed me to the Italian couple. After my adventures in the ghetto, I was ready for somewhere a bit less adventurous.

So off I went to meet Gloria and her husband, Joe, and to see the apartment. It was a bit dingy but had its own bathroom and a tiny stove. It even had a little window that I could peek through and watch the landlady's cat make its way through her vegetable garden. She and Joe were happy to get the extra money, and their son was only ten years old and rather quiet. I agreed to their rent price, and they gave me a key so I could feel safe at night. I moved in that weekend.

I used to hear them fighting every night, snarling at one another after supper. First she would call out sweetly to Joe, "Want some coffee, Joe?" and he would answer in his rough voice, "I'd love it."

Those were the last kind words I heard from them for the rest of the night. It was like listening to an old soap opera where the rule is "The louder, the better!" They were Italian and hot-tempered. I wondered if they knew I could hear them. Their son must have hidden out in his room, and was probably used to their wrangling.

In the meantime, I had more important things to worry about than the rocky relationship of my landlords. I knew that sooner or later I would have to explain myself to the superiors at the Motherhouse, but I had no words. How do you explain to people who are happy with most of the old-time rules and regulations that you need more independence? And that having more independence doesn't mean you are throwing the whole concept of convent life out the window? I needed time to get it all figured out and to be able to explain it to them in a way that they would understand and let me keep my gold ring and my vows, and most of all, the essence of my life as a nun. I don't know how I got so bold. It must have been memories of Rose's therapy, telling me every week to do it my own way, and in my own time. Somehow, I thought it would all work out. But of course it didn't!

I got a phone call from Mother Josepha at the Motherhouse, ordering me to come to see her the following Monday, to meet with several members of the Council regarding my concerns about community rules. That gave me plenty of hours that weekend to worry, and toss and turn all night, as well as to write down a few ideas to present when I reached the meeting. By the time I got there, I was so nervous I was sure I would lose my argument and would have to return to the traditional convent where I had been living before I happily dashed off to live in the slums for the past two adventure-filled years. I had relinquished my old room in that apartment, with a few tears on both sides, to its original owner. Now I had a new dwelling place that was suitable to me. I had to present it as equally suitable to the higher superiors who had never been comfortable with my vagabond wanderings from one place to another to live. I suppose the whole situation smacked of more independence than they were comfortable with. There was an edge of boldness in it that might have reminded Mother Josepha of my arguments with her long ago, when she told herself she had me under her thumb.

The meeting was not pleasant. They argued with me on the basis of the rules of the community that I had promised to uphold when I made my vows at the altar in front of the Bishop, my parents, the rest of my sisters who also made the same vows, and anyone else who happened to be in the chapel that long-ago day when we gave our lives to Jesus to do with however He chose. How innocent we were! We had such good intentions. Had I lost something spiritual during the years when I was pushing for my independence? I hoped not; it was a scary thought. Was I being asked to choose between what I considered to be obsolete rules of my convent and the Jesus to Whom I had vowed my life?

* * * * *

The worst part of that meeting was that some of the sisters who grilled me had known me when I was just a newly professed sister. They had helped me through many a hard time when convent life was incredibly rigid in so many awful ways. We had laughed together, then, at the ridiculousness of some of the requirements for our lives.

Now these same sisters did not understand why I wanted to change my life style.

I asked myself in a sudden panic, *Why am I asking for more? Do I really want to win this battle? Will the people that I have been friends with for so many years drop their friendships with me, and lose their feelings of closeness to me?*

I was the first one to speak. I gave the rationales for my desires to live on my own and still to be recognized as a nun like they were. We argued in the weird way that women, whether they are nuns or not, banter back and forth emotionally. We jumped from one issue to another and hoped that our opponent(s) would give in out of sheer exhaustion.

Mother Josepha was the most vehement. "What happened to the sacred vows you made at the altar, kneeling before the Bishop? You promised to uphold the rules of the community forever. And your parents were there, listening to your promises. Some of your sisters were there also, making the same vows. Have the others given them up also, like you are doing?"

How I wished Sister Olympia were there to defend me, but she was not a council member, and even if she had been what could she have said, other than that she understood my feelings and my desires for greater independence. She might have sensed if I could hang on for some more years, things would change and I could still wear my white robes, and live with sisters. But it was not to be, even if Sister Olympia had been there to talk on my behalf.

Did anyone understand why I wanted to change my life style? Even more painful than the Council Members' lack of understanding of my point of view, was my own feeling of more and more inferiority as the discussion raged on, in its nun-like way. No one raised her voice, but no one listened either. Each of us wanted her own argument to prevail. The only difference was that, if I gave in, my hope for a change in my lifestyle would be gone, probably for good. I would revert to a meek façade that wasn't me any longer, and hadn't been for quite a while.

The meeting ended in a debacle, with each side (and there was only me on my side) holding to their own beliefs. Before I gave up entirely, I quietly said, "Please listen to me. There are a few other sisters who have been living independently for several years in the same way in which I want to continue living. They have their own money, send the required amount to the motherhouse monthly and use the rest to take care of their rent, food, transportation, and sundry other needs. They are each working in their profession, making a living doing what they love. They have their own apartments, just like I do. The only difference is that they live in other states."

Suddenly, my self-control evaporated. I shouted furiously, "Doesn't the life-style of those other sisters bother you one bit? How come when I want to do it, it becomes a crime? Are you afraid that a few more sisters may want to do the same thing if they see me living alone in my own place in Queens or Brooklyn?" I was hoarse when I finished my tirade. The room was awash in an ugly silence. They never even answered my questions. My reasoning may not have made any sense to them.

The meeting ended there, with them suddenly re-assuring me as though I were having a nervous breakdown or were acting like a child in the midst of a tantrum. One sister even gently told me not to be bitter.

Bitter? I silently shouted. *I'm furious. There's a big difference between the two, in my book. Accusing me of being bitter is just one more insult.* But I said nothing. *Don't throw pearls before swine,* I advised myself grandly, although I was almost gasping from the effort to hold back my tears.

There was no real ending to our fruitless meeting. None of the salient issues had been resolved. Their bottom line was that I wasn't being the obedient nun that I had promised to be at the altar on the day of my vows. I understood their message. My return message was that I was not going to give up.

It's not as if I'm applying for a marriage license or looking for a boyfriend, I thought to myself. But my timing was all wrong. A number of years later, anyone who wanted to live on their own was allowed to, but by that time I was long gone, on to my own life, feeling "pushed out of the convent" because I wanted a new life style too early. What would I eventually have done if I had been "given my head" like farmers described one way to deal with an unruly horse? I only know that I wasn't handled the way I had hoped for.

I left the meeting room in tears. Ellen, one of my friends, had been pacing back and forth at the end of the hallway waiting for me to come out. She understood my distress like a true friend would. She knew two of the sisters that I had been talking about at the meeting who were living out of state on their own, each pursuing her own pathway. And she understood my dilemma. Her comfort was all I needed to keep on thinking about my own pathway and believing that it would all work out in the end. She herself left the community much later and found her place in life in another state. We still write and call each other and send hand-made birthday cards year after year, slipping in pictures of ourselves once in a while. We are much older now, but in the pictures we are still grinning with the same delight that we had when we first met in the novitiate more than 60 years ago.

For my part, I returned to my little apartment in Gotti land and continued my independent life. I enjoyed living on my own, despite the community's disapproval. Occasionally, one of the superiors brought me a shopping bag full of food and other necessities, and asked me how I was. She was a gentle soul; I felt somehow she was hoping I would capitulate. I thanked her as if the packages of Saltine crackers, wonderful cheeses and bags of dried fruit might persuade me to return to a dependent life. I shook my head after she left, almost throwing away the food in a kind of stupid rebellion.

I didn't need food; I could buy my own. The food gifts, without any mention of our battle at the Motherhouse just emphasized to me that they still didn't "get it." I wished I could reject her gift, keep my dignity, and not be branded rude. It was a balancing act. If Rose had been there she would have whipped out her jug of gin, and spread the crackers with that delicious cheese, chomping with delight, spraying little crumbs of cheese into the air.

"Don't be so grateful," Rose would have said. "They treated you meanly and here you are being humble about the whole thing." She was right, but years of being subservient are not readily washed away.

In the meantime, I had arranged my apartment just the way I wanted it. For the first time in many years I could arrange things without consulting other people. What a grand feeling! I bought a wooden rocker at a second-hand store and carried it all the way to my new little nest, stopping every block or so to put it down and catch my breath. I splurged on a bright orange cushion for the seat. I was thirty-six years old and the rocker was the first piece of furniture that I had ever purchased on my own. I treasured it. Things belonged to me. The dish drainer from the hardware store, the soap dish for the tiny bathroom, the few pots and pans piled into the stove—they were mine.

The saleswoman in the hardware store asked me if I had just gotten married and, blushing a little, I said "No, I'm just moving to a new part of town." Sometimes I sat in my chair watching the cat creep past the window and I said, "Thank you." I was so happy. I didn't care if the thank you drifted up to Jesus, or Buddha or whoever. I just wanted someone up there to know that I loved the way my life was working out.

Once in a while I had Ann and Therese come to visit. We were old friends and had battled the crazy rules together. We didn't agree with most of them, after all. We were like housewives cleaning out our closets and finding that a lot of the things that we loved the most somehow didn't fit us anymore. The question of whether we would still be traditional nuns continued to haunt us. Underneath our occasional rants, we still longed to devote our lives to God forever, just like we had when we were new young sisters. That had never changed despite our confusion and questioning.

After a while, we abandoned such serious discussions and relaxed. A bottle of Chianti wine, all wrapped round in a straw binding with a few fancy wine glasses nearby was on an old table next to my rocker. My friends and I sipped our wine, and toasted one another with the excitement of people who found themselves edging toward a new life. I used to have an occasional glass of wine when I was in the old-time convent, but never before in my own apartment.

What an exciting time this was! There was never a time equal to it. The euphoria was indescribable. I was a hostess in my own home, a queen without the tiara. Material things I didn't care about. The trappings could wait. I just wanted to get to the core of it all. Was this what Mother Josepha had been talking about when she prattled on and on about the joy of poverty? I doubted it.

I knew it would change in time, but for now it was what I wanted. The only thing that bothered me was the way the community kept trying to "understand" me as if I were a specimen under a microscope in a secret lab somewhere. Was I really so different? I had found my niche for the time being, and that was enough for me.

I FOUND A PART-TIME JOB

Before I secured my employment at the Board of Education, one other small job popped up. I decided to take it even though the pay was miniscule. The work was in a slum area in Brooklyn, near a majestic old church that was adjacent on one side to a food-stamp office and on the other to a run-down supermarket. The pastor of the church heard that I was a counselor and thought I could be helpful in working with his little gaggle of teen-agers whom he was trying to persuade to go to church more often. I wasn't so sure that I would be the best one to convince these straggly-haired, rough-looking kids to go to church, but—although I hadn't worked with teen-agers in a while—I decided to "give it a shot."

There were only eight youngsters in the group. They were as wary of me as I was of them. We used to meet in the school yard, me in my nondescript "modern" clothes that I had been using since we were able to go without our old habits, and them in whatever duds they had been able to battle their siblings for that morning. One girl in particular, Michelle, stood out. She wore a long ratty-looking black woolen coat the other kids made fun of. If I mentioned it, she glared at me. So I stopped asking about it.

One of the other teen-agers told me that Michelle lived with her blind grandmother in one of the projects and hadn't seen her mother, who lived in New Jersey, since last May when her mother got re-married. Gradually all the kids, except Michelle, told me bits and pieces about their lives. But Michelle kept to herself, other than showing up every morning to wander around the outskirts of the group and looking at me out of the corner of her eye.

These youngsters were eager to talk about anything but religion, which was why the pastor had brought me there. So I talked about their boyfriends, their parents, their teachers. When Carmela talked about the drunk who came home at night and kept her awake with his curses, I wondered whether he was her step-father, and worried whether he came to her bedroom. When Joey arrived at the morning meeting one day with an ugly looking bruise on his cheek, I asked him how he got it, and waited to hear either a made-up story, or something that sounded more reliable. There was no rushing this group. My hope was that the pastor would keep me long enough so they could reach a trust level with me. Then maybe they would go to church once in a while, and the pastor would keep me coming.

One morning while Michelle was wandering around at the edge of the group, I decided to take a chance and ask her about her grandmother.

"I'd like to say hello to her someday, Michelle," I said, not expecting an answer.

But she nodded and said, "You can only stay a few minutes." So the barrier was down! The next day, I climbed the stairs to the third floor of that ugly project and met a frail old lady who spilled out her worries as if she had been waiting all day just to tell them to someone, anyone.

Like the others had told me, Michelle resented her mother's new marriage dreadfully. She had begun wearing that long coat as soon as her mother left; the grandmother felt that Michelle was on the edge of falling prey to the evils of that benighted neighborhood. She was a sharp old lady and said the long coat was the way that Michelle was hiding from the world around her. She was as wise as a Yale therapist. The grandmother was not afraid to live alone there, but her inability to protect Michelle disturbed her terribly. So that was the story, and what was I to do? I needed a little time to think.

The pastor just wanted the teen-agers to go to church, and not do too much complaining about their miserable lives, lives which he couldn't fix, anyway. He had already made a few comments to me about how they were beginning to ask questions about church rules, especially about sex, and he wanted me to put a clamp on their thinking.

"You are teaching them to think," he said crossly one day, "and that's not why I hired you." I knew then, with a sad clarity, that my days working for him were numbered. If he had realized how many years it had taken me to think, he would have known why I thought it was natural for me to talk to kids about thinking.

I would have to work fast, if I were to help Michelle. Since the grandmother trusted me, I decided the two of us could persuade Michelle to go to Long Island, to a home for girls who were troubled. Some people at the courts told me the legal steps I should take, so I sat down with Michelle and her grandmother, and told Michelle she was on the brink of getting into a lot of trouble and the time to move to a boarding school way out on Long Island was now.

The funny thing was that she didn't argue with me; she just looked scared and stared at me until I touched her cheek and promised I would visit her once a month. "If you hate it after six months I will have you returned to your grandmother," I said. Her grandmother nodded in agreement as if I was a guru of some kind whose word was to be trusted, and the two of them stood up and went back to the miserable projects where they lived.

For someone like me who had never dealt with the courts before, it was a lot of promises, but I had a feeling of "now or never," and the grandmother agreed with me that waiting could end in disaster. Why Michelle trusted me I would never know, but she did. My contacts at the court warned me that we would have to wait for months for an appointment with the judge, but someone powerful made phone calls to someone else even more powerful and suddenly we had a quick date at Family Court. Michelle arrived swathed in her ratty, black winter coat. That, alone, would have persuaded any one on that sweltering July day that this was a girl who needed help. A legal guardian was appointed to save her from being bamboozled by some bossy person (like me) and I managed to warn Michelle, "If anyone asks you to say that you want to stay with your grandmother, tell them no."

True to form, the bustling legal guardian carrying her yellow note pad hurried over to Michelle three times and, with her back turned to me, asked Michelle some questions that I couldn't hear. I could see Michelle mouthing "No!" and I knew we had won. The judge called the grandmother to his desk and said Michelle would be moved to the Good Shepherd Home the following day. I watched from the shadowy church doors that morning as a nondescript car pulled up outside the grandmother's project and scooped up Michelle into its depths. She stuck her head out the window and seemed to be looking for someone, but I was afraid if I appeared she would holler that she had changed her mind.

For the next few months, I took the Long Island Railroad to Michelle's new home and watched a transformation slowly take place. She had a hard time, missed her grandmother and felt angry at me. But one dull November day, she ran out to meet me, carrying a large, clumsily-made teddy-bear that she had laboriously put together for me. One of the eyes was crooked and the mouth was sewn on with uneven stitches. I never repaired the bear's slipping features and I never gave him away.

Even better news, that day, was Michelle's excited tale of several talks that she had had with her mother and step-father and the plans that they were making for her to live with them by June. She was happy at the thought of finally leaving the Home and seemed surprisingly comfortable with the change.

"I'm doing good in school," she proudly declared. "I think I'm going to be a teacher!" I never knew if Michelle's dreams came true. I knew only that she had been saved in the nick of time from forever wandering in her long coat, always on the outskirts of society.

In the meantime, I unceremoniously got "fired" from my little job at the church. The pastor said I had not persuaded anyone to go to church and, worse yet, I had taught the kids to think. I didn't even defend myself. He said it as though it were a betrayal of his trust in me. I didn't know if I should say I was sorry. But of course I wasn't. I had helped Michelle and her grandmother, and that was enough for me. So I said goodbye to my gang of teen-agers, told them I loved them, and treated them to ice-cream with part of my last meager check. It was a low-key goodbye, but a sweet one.

I began to run low on money, and I knew it was time to use my connections in the Board of Education, where a friend told me they were looking for guidance counselors. With my certificate from the state proving my credentials, I trudged down to the local hiring office and applied for the job. The interviewer was worried that I would wear my religious outfit at work, but as soon as I promised that I would leave it hanging in the closet, I was immediately hired. As usual, my major concern was that I would have to speak Spanish, which, for some reason, constantly popped up as a job requirement just when I thought I had conquered all the tricky parts of a job interview.

My other concern was that I might be assigned to a well-to-do area. When I was in a modern neighborhood where there were upper-class buildings with uniformed doormen and sleek automobiles, I felt out-of-place. Where were the poor people, where were the semi-literate kids, where were the graffiti-decorated streets, and the cat-calls that I had come to accept as part of my morning walk to work? Where were the nitty-gritty causes that I had shared with other professionals as part of that work? If I wasn't there, I would miss it all. It had been the fabric of my life for a long time, the people, the misery, the suffering. There had been a kind of sad adventure to it all. My heart had gone out to the aching around me because I had felt aching in my own life for so long. I had wanted comfort for my own aches, and I had received it. And now I wanted a chance to give comfort to others. It took me a while to believe that going with the flow of life would deposit me in the right spot after all. The old convent lessons came through. "It will all work out in the end!" I told myself, and it did.

WHAT'S NEW, MARY? EVERYTHING!

To my relief, my Board of Education assignment was "city-wide." The term "city-wide programs" was a code to indicate specialized programs for autistic children, severely emotionally disturbed youngsters, aggressive teenagers who could not manage in regular classes, and various other young people all the way up to 21 years of age. I would work with youth of these types, in groups from one category or another, usually in poverty-stricken areas where the principal had a few extra classrooms that could be used for these children. Sometimes an entire school was set aside for such youngsters.

So I had my job and I had my apartment; now I needed a car. My brother found me a used 1967 Pontiac for the princely sum of $500. It had started out with eight cylinders but, as time went on, that eventually sank down to a pitiful four. When I told the Motherhouse that I had bought a car, they wanted me to send them my full salary each month. They assured me that they would send me whatever money I needed the minute that I asked. I felt awkward as usual, but I refused.

I saw in them my own naïveté that had been part of me for so many years. Now I was explaining to them how the real world worked.

"The mechanic won't release my old wreck of a car after it is repaired unless I pay him the day that I pick up the car," I said calmly. I was more adult than they were. I already sent them the usual substantial stipend every month, but I kept the rest for my own ordinary needs, like rent and food. I was tired of explaining myself when I thought my reasoning was logical. They didn't try to persuade me again. Maybe one of the superiors had a brother who was a mechanic somewhere, and told them how the world of car repair worked, or that milk could not be paid for with a smile.

But the car was not my only problem. I had to learn how to drive. I decided to enroll in a driving school rather than ask my brother to teach me. After my first lesson with the driving school teacher, he started sweating as soon as I got in the car and cursed under his breath on a regular basis. After the first few lessons he told me stories about other students who had been even worse drivers than I was. I hated those little stories, but I was afraid to complain.

"Slow down," he yelled. "Your car is going to land in the trunk of another car!" Sometimes he dredged up a horrible tale about a woman who threw a suicide note out the car window, was hit by a new driver such as me, and subsequently died in the street. I should have been insulted that he spent his time telling me these stories because I was paying for my lessons and had all I could do to concentrate on my driving, but I was afraid he would tell the driving school that I was incapable of ever getting my license. So instead I signed up for extra lessons.

His approach reminded me of a technique that was used in the convent, when we were just beginning to teach. Every other week, we met with an older sister who told us wildly fabricated stories about a trolley car man who informed her of the faults and failings of some imaginary sister who had ridden on his trolley. I believed all those stories then (even though most of the other sisters didn't) and I believed my driving instructor, too.

Finally, the official from the Motor Vehicles Department met me at the driving school to accompany me to the site where I would take my formal driving test. My teacher had apparently hoped that I could manage as long as I remembered all his platitudes, so he told the official that I was ready to take the test. But I wasn't. I drove right through a red light. My second test required that I park the car. But the other cars were too close to mine, and I snuggled up to another car far too close for comfort. My third test was a success. I received my license and was able to get myself where I needed to be. I never did develop a real sense of direction and I had a dreadful time getting around the five boroughs, but like most other things in my life I finally succeeded. It was kind of like getting a bi-lingual license. No one, including myself, believed I could get either a driver's license or a bi-lingual license, but I got both of them.

I drove my old wreck of a car back to the local hiring office where I first met the kindly man who had told me there was a job waiting for me. He had me sign some important- looking papers, and told me I would be starting in two weeks. I was ecstatic at my accomplishments. I had my driver's license, my job, my apartment and all kinds of dreams for my future. What a good life I had!

Most of my friends worked in crime-ridden neighborhoods like I did and labored with the lower echelons of society, so we had a real comradeship when we met. Sandy, a really classy lady, who was a gentle soul, taught the women prisoners at Riker's Island how to read, and passed through guard after guard to reach her classroom safely. I never worked with Sandy but we were friends for many years, and helped one another to understand the forces that pushed and pulled those women in and out of prison. Learning to read was the least of the women's problems, but Sandy tried her best to treat them as human beings and not simply as illiterate failures in life.

Maddy, in pursuit of her doctorate in social psychology, worked with teen-agers who lived in a mental institution but were allowed to come to a special Bronx school as a form of rehabilitation. She wanted me to work with her and so I ended up in that environment where, for some unknown reason, I felt comfortable.

* * * * *

The Bronx school was actually an old garage where the re-cycled air still smelled vaguely of gasoline. It was a strange-looking building where the classrooms were isolated from one another. The kids liked it because it didn't look like a school, and the teachers didn't really care how it looked as long as the janitor swept the floor at the end of the day. If someone asked me where I worked, I used to say with a laugh, "I work in a garage." We left as a group when the day was over, because the neighborhood was too dangerous for us to walk alone.

One time, I went into a store next door to the school before class started, and made the mistake of putting my dollar bill on the counter so I could pick up my coffee cup. It was gone in a flash. Lesson learned! I got a scolding from the lady behind the coffee counter on how to manage myself in her shop, shaking her head in annoyance that I was so unaware of what constituted smart behavior in her neighborhood. I felt embarrassed as if I had failed a basic lesson in how to live. "Go back to your own neighborhood," she seemed to say, "and don't blame us if you are careless around money. You're not living on Fifth Avenue." I slunk back to the school, and drank my coffee silently.

The kids knew how to handle themselves better than we did. On my first day in the South Bronx school, one of the boys jumped up, locked the door to the classroom, and shouted to his classmates, "Let's rape her." How nice. What a lovely greeting. I said in my old-time nun-voice, "Sit down." Then I unlocked the door. I think the other youngsters were scared by him; they were grateful someone was in charge and I was grateful and a little surprised that it was me. I heard later that he had been released from the psychiatric ward the day before. Once I got used to being surrounded by rather frightening kids, I enjoyed going there. The staff was professional and my car was safe in those surroundings, because apparently no one wanted it. One of the teachers used to leave a few old hamburger wrappers and an empty pretzel bag on the seat, hoping that the messiness would discourage any thief. I doubted it, but he had worked there for five years, so I decided he knew more than I did. When I drove my car back to my little home in Queens, I felt triumphant. One more obstacle overcome for the day!

My charmed life almost came to an end when my temporary license had to be changed to a regular license if I were to continue to work at the Board of Education. The licensing clerk curtly informed me that the only license test being given was for bi-lingual guidance positions. "The deadline for applications is today at five o'clock, and I'm not missing my train because of late-comers!"

"But I can't speak Spanish," I protested weakly.

"Missy," she said, "Fill out this application and give it to me today! And don't forget about the $15 application fee. The Bank closes in ten minutes. And learn Spanish!"

So I ran across the street to the bank, got the money order, and rushed back to the clerk's office. If she hadn't bossed me around like that, I wouldn't have had a chance at taking that exam and probably wouldn't have gotten the only job I was qualified for. The clerks in the Board of Education saved my career more than once, crossly reminding me that they were trying to get home and would I please hurry up. You had to be brave to work in the Board of Education. The clerks acted like the bossiest Mothers Superior you ever met, but they knew their business and they "pulled my bacon out of the fire" many a time, because they knew the ropes. Luckily, I learned instant obedience years ago when I was in the novitiate.

Once, when I had got different directions from one clerk after another, one of them said, "Do what I tell you and go home." I did what she said, and in the end I got my bi-lingual license, after the usual trauma of pretending that I could speak Spanish.

The licensing test was given a few weeks later in Brooklyn, in a huge high school where the classrooms were packed with women chatting excitedly in Spanish. I lowered my eyes as if I was back in the convent meditating and did not want to be disturbed. Actually I could not understand a word they were saying. When the written part of the test was finished, I waited nervously until my name was called for the interview section.

The English part of the test had been heavily directed to psychology and this meant that I had been able to answer most of the questions with relative ease. I even managed to write the obligatory essay in Spanish. I used only the present tense and stopped as soon as I reached the magic number of words demanded by the test instructions. The final part of the test consisted of a trio of unsmiling men who asked me some interview questions. They had the grace to look stunned when I used my meager supply of Spanish vocabulary words over and over again. I could understand the questions, but I was so scared that I forgot almost my entire vocabulary. They nodded politely when I finished floundering through my interview. One of the men told me that I would receive my score in a few weeks.

There was a security guard outside the classroom checking the names of the examinees off a long list of applicants. He said to me kindly, "You have to come back this afternoon to take the interview test for Elementary School, Bi-lingual Counselor."

I almost shouted at him, "I'm not coming back."

He looked at me sadly, as if I needed counseling myself. "But that test you just took was for high school counselors. If you passed that one, you will probably pass the one this afternoon."

I just shook my head, and smiled at him. I didn't go back.

A few weeks later, I got a postcard in the mail, giving me the amazing news that I had passed with a 65% and had my license as a bi-lingual counselor. I discovered later that most of the women, who had scared me half-to-death chattering in fluent Spanish, had not passed the English part of the test. The city had to give another test to meet their quota of bi-lingual counselors. But my license qualified me forever.

There is a God, I said to myself, *and He speaks all languages.*

By the end of the week, I received my assignment to a school that needed a bi-lingual Spanish-speaking counselor. I made a frantic phone call to my boss who knew that my Spanish was not job-worthy. She transferred me to a special residence for out-of-control teenage boys who had been placed there by the courts as a last resort in lieu of jail. They had the saddest stories imaginable, but once again the staff was professional and I was able to manage the group, mainly because I could supply innovative additions to their classes. I dreamed up all kinds of ways to prepare them for job interviews. That gave the teachers a break once a week, because I taught the ten-minute class while the teachers sat in the back of the room and took those few minutes off. The whole idea of those boys getting real jobs was ridiculous because they already had long records for stealing, beating up their girlfriends, assaulting old people, using their fists, knives, or bats on anyone who embarrassed or bothered them. Only stores in a poor area would know how to handle them and probably wouldn't even let them in the door, because they knew the boys couldn't be trusted. They needed years of anger management even to live normally. It was a pathetic situation.

It was hard not to get attached to some of these vulnerable youngsters, but mostly I was just there to take my cues from the teachers who were far more experienced with them than I was. I did whatever the teachers asked of me. I cared about those teen-agers, all of us did, but there was very little we could do. One of the boys had raped his mother. I was duly warned, and I talked to him with the door of my so-called office always open, and a teacher in the hallway. It was not a job from which you went home at the end of the day full of good feelings about the successes you had had.

My boss used to say "Watch your back and try to give a kid a good day if you can. Give him a few minutes when he is listened to and face the fact that you can't do much more." She was a wise woman. She set the bar low and the worse the boy's prognosis was the lower the bar went. It helped all of us to be realistic and not so impatient with these rough teenagers whose lives were already blighted far beyond any piddling problem we might have had in our own lives.

The first day that I went to the residence, Daryll, one of the new boys, sashayed over to me with his tee-shirt tied under his pectoral muscles as if it was a blouse. He had red nail polish on, and he greeted me with a flimsy hand shake. The staff told me they tried to make the homosexual boys dress less provocatively in order not to arouse fights among them. At Christmas time, the staff had a party for all the kids, and anyone who wanted to sing a song or tell a joke could do so. Daryll sang a popular song by Morris Albert, called "Feelings," one of those moon-y songs that were intended to touch your heart. Maybe when it was crooned by one of the popular singers at the time it got tiresome, but when Daryll, who had multiple problems and was trying to find someone to love and be loved by, sang it, the song took on new proportions. Hearing him sing it kind of ripped my heart.

A few years after I had left that residence, I was riding on the subway and saw Daryll slip into the car. He shouted out, "Miss Hughes!" and ran over to me to give me a hug and a kiss. I was so glad to see him, still alive, not knifed on a street somewhere, not dead from AIDS. A few of the passengers looked shocked and moved away from me, but I felt relieved that Daryll was still with us. I had been fond of him. I remember that hug and kiss even now after so many years.

Sometimes, if the teacher thought a boy was ready for a real job, I took the boy to a job interview. I waited outside the fast-food joint and accompanied him back to the residence where the boys lived, and hoped for the best. If he lost the job, he waited for me at the door of the residence the next day, with a few choice curses for me. It was not an easy job, ever. But then my efforts at being a nun had not been traditional nor had my life. It was all good in my book. I had no complaints. This was work I wanted to do, in the areas of the city where I wanted to earn my living. At the end of the day, I wanted to hustle back to my own apartment and relax, not read the Bible, not say the rosary, not pray. Just put my feet up and think about my day.

The Motherhouse continued to contact me with the hope that I would change my mind. I continued to "stick to my guns," which—come to think of it—was an appropriate phrase to use, given my work!

DONE IN BY A WATER BUG

Why did I go back to the old brick convent after I had fought so hard to live on my own? Did the Motherhouse finally persuade me to return to the fold? Or was it the sudden realization that other inhabitants were living in the basement apartment of which I thought I was the sole tenant? Horrors! I was sharing my humble quarters with stealthy water bugs that apparently came out only at night. I glimpsed one of those many-legged inhabitants when I was having trouble sleeping one evening and I glanced up at the ceiling. He was walking in a sprightly manner directly over my bed. Ugh! At any moment, he could drop down on my pillow. That was the end of my living in a basement apartment.

The next morning, I rushed to my landlady and told her I was moving out as soon as I could.

She stared at me as she asked, "Didn't you know that water bugs live in the basement?"

Of course I didn't know! Cockroaches, I knew about from New York City apartments. But not water bugs. Now that I had made their acquaintance, I had to leave the basement to them. I felt squeamish about bugs anyway. And I could manage to live in a convent again for a while until I decided what I wanted to do with myself.

I wrote my landlady a generous check to cover two weeks, and then drove directly to the Motherhouse to tell Mother Josepha I was coming home. I knew they would accept me for a while, until I had a viable plan, in whatever convent had an empty bed. . When Mother Josepha heard my reason, vis-à-vis water bugs, she just shook her head, pursed her lips and muttered a few platitudes that sounded familiar from novitiate days. She had always thought I was odd, but the authority she enjoyed holding over me had mercifully been chipped away by the changes in the rules the past few years. Just in case she might still need a final push toward giving me what I wanted, I gave her a phony smile like the ones she had given me so many years ago. I wanted her to feel that I didn't mind if she was still in charge. In the end we would both win, and we knew it. What a strange ending after all the angst we had endured so many years ago in the novitiate. Maybe she was glad to have me back, where she wouldn't have to explain to the other superiors why I was once again under her wing, so to speak.

Luckily, the Motherhouse was always ready to help its errant members back into the fold. Their acceptance required I give up a few of what I knew they would regard as some of my more outrageous demands. The mere thought gave me a comfortable feeling that I would at least have general membership in the community. Like an heirloom that had been discovered in an old corner of the attic, I would be assigned to a convent, where I would be welcome once again, provided I fit into the general atmosphere and didn't make everyone else feel as if they were out of place.

I planned to continue to work with the unruly adolescents in Brooklyn in order to "earn my keep" as the old-fashioned phrase put it. The work suited me, and paid well. The nightly return to the old, but comfortable, convent where there were still sisters who welcomed me pleased me. The dog wagged his tail when I wandered into his corner. I waited peacefully for my next plan to evolve.

The tribulations with the Motherhouse subsided, which was a relief for me and for them. I saw my friends frequently and kept my rattle-trap of a car and even some of my money, because it was clear that the car could die at any time. Besides, I wanted to have some extra cash in case something popped up that I really wanted to do. Things seemed to be moving smoothly, but, underneath it all, I knew that my life was on a path toward change. The Motherhouse knew it too and had given up trying to figure me out.

I got two interesting phone calls during the first summer after I returned to the traditional convent. One was from my sister, Peggy, who lived in Chicago and wanted me to spend a week or so with my three teen-age nephews. They had been nagging her to let them remain with their father in a hippie commune in Tennessee. Two of the hippies had come to visit Peggy that very week. They struck her as fine people, but she needed a "spy" who could tell her how life was lived there. It would have been awkward if she had suddenly appeared in the commune.

I remember saying "Peggy, it's not like going down to the corner store to buy a quart of milk." I knew that in the end I would go to that commune to check it out for her. At the same time, I could have a free-and-easy visit with my nephews.

Life was much looser in the convent by that time. A visit to the commune could be described as charity towards my nephews. My meager bank account would meet the requirements of a short trip to Tennessee. Besides, superiors were not as rigid as they used to be, especially if you were paying your own way.

The other phone call was from my old pal, Imelda. Her sense of humor had saved me from living in unbearable confusion when I tried to make sense out of my first teaching assignment in Brooklyn. She wanted me to go with her on a short vacation to Puerto Rico that summer, but we agreed that waiting until the next summer would fit more easily into both of our schedules.

Each of these trips would have a profound influence on my life, although I didn't realize it at the time.

DISCOVERY OF LIFE IN A COMMUNE

The trip to the commune took first priority, so I made my airline reservations, packed a small bag, and left my religious robes and veils in the convent in Queens, with a bemused superior shaking her head.

Off I flew to Nashville, where I was met promptly at the airline terminal by two bearded hippies in a red pick-up truck waving delightedly at me, a nun in secular disguise. My three young nephews dangling over the backboard of the truck added further local color to the scene. It was a glorious ride to the commune, filled with wild snippets of conversation and constant interruptions by each of us who wanted desperately to include their latest bit of news before it was swallowed up by the cheerful shouts of the other passengers.

Our first stop at the commune itself was like a picture out of a biblical story-book. Steven, the founder and guru of the commune, leaned against a large leafy tree in a half-sitting, half-lying position. His followers gathered around him and listened to a talk that engrossed them. He smiled at me and motioned me to come closer. It was an amazing introduction. Any number of quotations from the Bible could have been inserted into that scene. The guru's quiet tones continued. The occasional assent breathed by the followers punctuated the little spaces in his talk. And even I, who had just taken a long trip to reach him and his commune, did not think to interrupt whatever was going on in that bubble of concentration that was so different from the formal meditations that I had struggled through for years in the convent chapel. As I listened to him, peace gently descended upon me; and, although I had not yet unearthed any insights that I could bring back to my sister, I felt instinctively that the boys were safe.

My nephews, who were accustomed to the guru and his gatherings of followers by his pulpit-tree, had correctly assumed that I was quite comfortable in my new surroundings. They proceeded to escort me with all the aplomb of bell-hops to my sleeping quarters. That part of Tennessee was desperately hot in the summer months, so some of the housing at the commune was completely open on all sides. My sister, who had never seen a picture of the commune, probably imagined that the sleeping arrangements would at least have walls separating little cubicles so that a degree of privacy could be assured.

But there were no cubicles, no walls, no privacy at all. There were only foam-rubber mattresses and sheets casually spread upon them. I climbed the steps to the huge wooden platform with only a whispered question to my nephew, "Do the men sleep here too?" He pointed obligingly to a second platform for single men a few feet away. I breathed a sigh of relief. I didn't want to sleep on a platform with men. It would have embarrassed me. I was still very much a nun. I left my satchel next to an unused mattress, and wandered a bit with my nephews, who were eager to introduce me to their friends. One of their married friends invited me to their home for the evening meal and brought me there just as the sun went down.

Five adults and three small children crowded into the living room to meet me and share a few hours of comradeship with me. Their warmth and friendliness was a hallmark of this lovely commune where I found it so easy to feel at home.

One of the wives was quite pregnant and when her husband came into the living room he greeted her with a gentle kiss and then with a little pat to her belly. It was a gesture that I found endearing and unselfconscious. I never forgot it.

My attempts at smoking a marijuana cigarette that evening resulted in my collapse into happy giggles. It was the first time that I had ever puffed on any kind of cigarette, marijuana or otherwise, and I felt guiltily proud of myself as if I had entered the world of grown-ups at last. One of the women looked at me kindly and said, "The marijuana is affecting you, isn't it?" I felt a little annoyed at her, as if she meant that one cigarette had turned me into an addict. It was the whole commune that was affecting me, not just the few puffs of marijuana.

It was hard for me to sleep that night when I returned to my mattress, my sheet, and my untouched satchel. A window had opened for me. There were monastic rules I had surrounded myself with for years that I had never fully accepted in my heart. Part of me had been gently changing over time, and the ease with which I slid into the commune philosophy brought the shifts in attitude home to me in a more comfortable way than any tutorial would have done during a formal religious retreat. I decided to immerse myself in commune living and analyze whatever was happening to me after I returned to the convent.

For several days, I wholeheartedly followed the general farm schedule, which consisted of weeding the long rows of potatoes, tomatoes, and various other crops that were raised by the commune members. It was hard work and gave me an appreciation of the effort needed if one is going to obtain fresh vegetables. My sister never mentioned that my surveillance duties at the commune would involve so much manual labor. But I had an exciting time, far from the convent routine, and decided to tease her about whatever she had forgotten to mention when I returned to convent life.

I was assigned to the same farm team every morning and worked with a friendly group of three young women, only a few years younger than I. As we weeded, we traded innocent jokes, complained about the heat, and cheerfully offered the water jug to one another. There was a familiar comradeship among us that reminded me of the convent.

Suddenly I noticed a young red-haired man frequently glancing at me with a sweet smile. I felt edgy immediately.

What is the matter with you? I said to myself.

I looked around and saw that the women on my team had already started another row of tomatoes. I hurried to move closer to them. I hadn't felt this anxious since I left the novitiate, where the smallest thing managed to make me a nervous wreck. Back then I was always afraid of making a mistake, and now that same feeling of uncertainty hung over me. I unexpectedly remembered a boy I had worked with from a mental institution who had been given a pass to visit his family and found a note on the apartment door saying, "We moved."

He ran back to the mental hospital and banged on the door begging to be let in again.

Had I moved interiorly? Was I in a setting that I was halfway drawn to? Did I belong in the convent or in a mixed group of men and women?

I began to blurt out my feelings to my team members, feelings that I had not recognized before.

"I feel so nervous when a man acts as if he likes me," I said fearfully. Without analyzing me as if Freud's disciples had suddenly materialized in a Tennessee potato field, they suddenly became like older sisters. They said all the right things.

"We will be with you all day, and tomorrow too!" they said to reassure me. I felt loved and protected. The red-haired man worked in a different field the next day and, even if he had worked right next to me, I would have managed to control my nervous feelings. I felt safe from anything for which I was not ready. Did I like that red-haired man? Yes, but the time for me to be attached to a man was in the distant future. Like the psalms say, "There is a time for everything under the sun," and the potato fields of a commune were not the place for even the most innocent kind of romance to enter my life.

Am I afraid of men? I asked myself later. I did not know the answer, but the question bothered me for months.

I decided not to spend all my time weeding crops with the other hippies. I was curious about the philosophy of the commune, and spent blocks of time listening to the guru, asking him questions and thinking about his answers. Unlike retreat priests or overbearing superiors, he did not attempt to shape my beliefs. I tucked away some of his viewpoints to contemplate later when I was alone in my convent chapel. It was too much to absorb all at once. I needed to be alone to sort it out.

Much like the convent, there were many shared activities. One of these activities was doing laundry with several other women in a huge room filled with tubs of steaming hot water and loaded with clothing of all sorts. When I first entered the laundry room, I had my clothing on, despite the fact that the other women had discarded all their garments in tribute to the brutally hot temperature in the room. They suggested to me that I do the same, and I declined in a rather horrified tone. Five minutes later, I was naked as the day I was born, without a bit of hesitation. Five minutes after that Eve-like exposition, in came my 15-year old nephew and, to his credit, he did not even give his old auntie a second glance, other than a rather startled expression when he first saw me in all my glory. I washed all his clothes, which he had brought into the laundry room in a bulky bag, and he never mentioned the laundry room again. I was not surprised at myself that I didn't mention my laundry strip-tease to my sister. The story belonged in the commune, where it would be looked on as practical and nothing else.

My sister, who was as fussy as I was about privacy, forgot to tell me that there were no indoor toilets at the commune. Instead, there were small wooden out-houses with no doors, set on high hills overlooking the beautiful green fields, so you did not breathe in odors other than the natural farm scents. It did not occur to me to worry when there was a man sitting in the two-holer cubicle next to mine. I was separated from him by a slender wooden plank. We talked comfortably about my day and what I thought about the commune. It was not a picture that you would find on a travel brochure. Yet, even today, memories of those green hills and those friendly out-houses still give me a happy feeling. What was it about the commune that made me feel so relaxed in the midst of an environment that was so different from anything I had known for most of my life? I never quite figured it out.

Occasionally, during my last few days at the commune, I decided what I really saw was a live enactment of the Acts of the Apostles, where the early Christians held all things in common.

Later, when I returned to the convent, someone asked me, "Did you teach them anything?" I immediately felt angry at the bland ignorance of that statement and answered furiously, "They are living the gospel of Jesus!"

The most dramatic event of my commune adventure was the Sunday morning meeting at which the guru presided. Trying to describe that meeting adequately to anyone who had not experienced it was impossible. I had photographs, but I captured the essence of the experience in my soul, not on paper. The guru stood in a shaded spot, with hundreds of his followers seated around him. Little children played near their parents, and my nephews and I grinned at each other as though we had just found the finest picnic spot in the world, with the best people with whom to share it. Weddings were performed that morning, problems aired and discussed, pot smoked, joy abounded. It was a glorious morning and one that I never forgot.

One evening a musical event occurred in the fields. Spontaneous dancing, wild whirling, and singing went on for a few hours. I watched the dancers, especially one young woman dressed in an orangey swirl of gauzy material. She looked like a sunset come to earth. Her freedom was attractive, her body kept pace with the music. I watched her, longed to find the same freedom within myself, and wondered if I ever would.

What's going on with you, Mary? I asked myself.

But the answer didn't come while I was at the commune. It was too soon. It would have broken me apart in its ferocity.

Wake up, wake up, Mary!

But I didn't know I wanted to wake up. When the awakening came, I moved, with the same suddenness that marked my blurting out feelings in the potato field to women I barely knew. There was no hesitation then, nor was there any when it was time for me to break loose and go to a new life. A line in Scripture said it clearly for me, "You will shake off the dust from your sandals and move to a new dwelling in that day." And I did so with great joy when my moment came.

I never told my sister the impact that the commune had on me. It was too intimate an experience. There were parts about the commune that I loved and parts that scared me, and I think she knew that. She kept her distance respectfully. I wondered why I was so careful about sharing myself, but I was. It was the only way that I could finally grow up, calm within myself.

My sister died five years later. My last visit with her had its usual mixture of love and slight irritation. I looked at her as she sat in her lounge chair with an oxygen tank beside her.

"Peggy," I said. "I can't believe this is happening to you."

She simply nodded her head as if there were no answer to give to me or to anyone. I realized in that instant that words were no longer necessary between us. Our relationship was complete.

I went to the commune to help my sister at a desperate time in her life, but in a strange way my helping her slowly propelled me into looking at a different lifestyle myself. Like an unknowing guide, she had walked with me on that quiet pathway, each of us seeking our own truth. As they say in the Jewish religion, it was a mitzvah.

When I returned to the convent, I wanted to tell everyone about my experiences in the commune, but something told me not to chance talking about my adventures to sisters who might laugh at the wrong times, or tighten their lips in disapproval.

An old Biblical admonition kept popping into my head, "Don't throw your pearls before swine." I read every pamphlet I could find about new ways of worshipping God, but I never talked about the Sunday morning meetings with the guru and his followers. I could find nothing, in any of the thick books that used to give me comfort in the old days, that lifted my spirits like living at the commune did. I finally decided that I was thinking too much, trying too hard.

I told myself that Jesus could not possibly expect from me what I had thought He wanted for so many years. My anxiety over pleasing Him was slowly seeping out of me. I began to feel like a carefree kid again, like I had felt before I first pinned on my filmy black veil and declared to my neighbors that I was entering the convent. What I really wanted now was to be living alone in my own cramped but pretty apartment like I had been doing before the water bug intruded on my life. I wanted to work where people needed me, pray when I felt like it, have time with my friends, eat out once in a while, keep on studying, and have a little bit of money.

Sometimes I asked myself, *Do I want to leave the convent?*

But even the words "leave the convent" made me nervous. Those vows I had made long ago were still so much a part of me. They could not be comfortably shaken off. Whatever changes lay in wait for me, I was not ready for them. Maybe I never would be.

PUERTO RICO AND THEN THE WORLD!

*G*oing to Puerto Rico so soon after visiting the hippie commune will be more a chance to sit back and relax than it will be a learning experience, I happily told myself. *I'll be in the tropics, baking in the sun and occasionally dipping my toes in the warm water. Besides, I'll be with Ann, my old pal from the early days in the convent. What could be better?*

So I gleefully packed my bags and met Ann at the airport, ready to relax. I had forgotten how she always came with an agenda whenever we got together, and usually there were multiple parts to that agenda that I never foresaw. Sure enough, she tossed a surprise into our plans, cheerily announcing it with a big grin.

"The first place we'll visit will be the country home of two of my old friends, Jose and Maria Garcia. They'll take one look at us and offer us a bath," Ann said with a twinkle in her eye.

"You're kidding me, aren't you?" I protested weakly. "I can't take a bath in a stranger's house!" But the sweat rolling down my back was destroying my resistance.

Ann gave me the same grin that she had given me long ago when she told me that Sister Waltruda got our welcome cake from Subic's day-old bakery. She was laughing at me, and I knew it. I always had a bit of the proper lady in me. All of a sudden, it was okay to have someone poke fun at me like in the old days. The bathwater was cool and refreshing and the family was so nonchalant about sharing their home that I actually felt at ease.

I heard Ann chattering away in Spanish in the living room, and I managed to catch a few words here and there. I began to unwind and feel that this would be a really great trip. Later, as we sat and ate the simple meal that the family provided, I wondered to myself if I would ever want to live in Puerto Rico. Ann had lived there for a few years and loved the language, the people, the culture. But I had always resisted drastic changes in my life. Sister Waltruda, with all her weirdness, had been more than enough change for me. I just wanted to plod along in an ordinary life.

My little reverie was interrupted by Ann, who asked me if I wanted to visit some of the convents where she had friends. I wasn't too eager, but I hadn't made a fuss about visiting other convents when we were planning this trip, so I felt I had to go along.

She was excited, not only to see her friends, but also to introduce me to each and every one of them. Inside, I groaned. I was social, but not as quick as Ann to mingle with a lot of people. I really wanted to see Puerto Rico with all its lush growth and beautiful beaches. Meeting every sister in Puerto Rico was not my idea of a vacation.

Oh dear, I thought. *How did I ever get into this?*

But I loved Ann, so I said nothing. I just decided that the next time I went somewhere with anyone I would make more inquiries before I bought my ticket.

The vacation wore on. I sweated through all my clothes, mumbled privately a lot, and wished I had thought more carefully when I agreed to go away to such a hot and humid place. But the laughter that Ann and I shared, and the old stories, made us both happy in that special way that true friends treasure.

Toward the end of the two weeks, as I went into my fifth convent and greeted group after group of lively sisters, I began to think about what it would be like to live the rest of my convent life as an old nun.

Why am I thinking that? I questioned myself. But the answer was staring me in the face. Old nuns, too fragile to go out much, fingered their rosaries and looked at me, the stranger in their midst who probably provided the only splash of excitement in their day. The young nuns ran in and out, did their work, prepared their lessons for the next day's teaching, chatted to each other, or maybe meditated silently as they paged through a book of Latin prayers.

But old nuns, I thought to myself, *are stuck in a quiet prayerful life, and this is not what I want. I don't want to be under the control of someone who determines where I will live. I don't want to spend my life praying the rosary. I am too young. I love God, but I need activity and action and change. I want a self-determined life. And I need money to arrange my destiny as far as I am able. A few sticks of furniture and a little place of my own will be enough for me, and oh yes, a telephone so I can call all my friends.*

That was the moment when I knew I was leaving the convent. The die was cast. The decision that I hadn't known brewed in me had risen to the surface. I didn't tell Ann that day. I didn't tell anyone. I quietly made my plans and smiled a lot and worried about how I would tell my mother. That would be my next hurdle, but I would deal with it when the time came. Ann and I said goodbye to everyone, packed our bags and boarded the plane back to New York.

When I reached New York, I wrote my letter to the Bishop and told him that I wanted to be released from the vows I made 24 years before. He was in no hurry to give me permission to leave the religious life. Maybe he hoped I would change my mind. While I waited for his response to my letter, I had fun picturing little printing press in the basement of the elite home of the Bishop. The letters of release rolled off the presses like in the movies, where significant news bulletins caused groans of distress or gasps of excitement from on-lookers who wondered what was happening to their world.

But my world was changing, too, as I quietly anticipated the end of an era in my own life. A Bishop who cared might try to keep me in the convent for a few more years. In the end, the result would be the same. This was no longer the life for me.

Two months later the official letter came. It was a cold, distant missive. Until it was signed and notarized by one of the superiors from the Motherhouse, in my presence, it had no legal standing as far as the community having a right to any monies I made while I was in the convent. The letter itself gave me the right to lead my life however I chose. I could live separately, search for someone to date for a week or so, move on to another man with whom I felt comfortable. How I would find these men was not yet in my imagination. I kept my copy of the Bishop's letter for a long while, in my handkerchief drawer. Every so often I compared the number of years I spent in the convent with the time I now spent on my own. When the "outside" years caught up to the "inside" years, was I supposed to say a little prayer over the letter and bury it deeper I my handkerchief drawer? Would that mean that that part of my life was over? Somehow, I felt as confused as ever, but at least my next step was up to me.

The same mimeographed letter probably was sent to every sister who asked to be released from her vows. I didn't think the Bishop cared much about the nuns. They were a bother, always wanting to change things. Priests who wanted to leave the clerical life were hauled off for long interviews with the Bishop, who tried to convince them to wait for a while. The Bishop wanted priests to remain in the service of the Church. Anything to keep the priest in the Church.

I remembered learning in catechism classes when I was a youngster that, when a priest was ordained, a mark was put on his soul that remained there forever. I was quite impressed by the story of that mark. The mark glowed if the priest went to Heaven; it burned if he went to Hell. But it was always there.

I finally told the Superior that I would leave as soon as I got an apartment. Ann, who had left the convent a few years earlier, knew someone who had put an ad in the church bulletin asking for a "Good Irish girl" who wanted to rent an apartment near the local parish church. I wanted to rent that apartment desperately, and I was certainly Irish, but was I still Good if I had left the convent? I wondered if the landlady would want to know my background and if she would watch to see if I entertained an occasional man in that little apartment. I signed the handwritten lease that my new landlady finally offered me and tucked it into an old prayer book that I knew I would never outgrow.

I continued to live in the old convent for several weeks while I arranged everything in my new little apartment. Then I told the sisters still living in the old stone convent what I was doing. They seemed to have guessed that I wanted to leave. I wondered if they were a little troubled to see one more of their formerly tight-knit group breaking loose.

But I, I bubbled with happiness as I stepped into a new life. I had not realized how long I had wanted to make this change. I remembered a saying from Juliana, an ancient saint. She had a vision one day, while she was praying. Jesus came to her and said, "All will be well, all will be well, all will be most well." I liked it. I didn't have to analyze it. I didn't have to ask some old priest what it meant. I didn't have to meditate on it every day. Maybe I would remember it when I was on my deathbed. Maybe I wouldn't. Who cared! All will be well. That was all I had to remember.

A few weeks later, I went to see my mother and told her I was leaving the convent. I had been so worried that she would be upset. Instead, she made a fist and raised her wrinkled old arm in a bold kind of revolutionary salute.

"Anything for your freedom," she said. She was joyful. She was celebrating. She didn't care what her friends would say, or worry about how I would manage as I worked my way through a whole new life. She would always be there for me, rooting for my freedom. She was my wonderful mother. She was my freedom fighter and always had been.

The final steps to freedom were stirring in me. With my official letter from the Bishop, I was free to begin dating. An interim boyfriend popped up, someone that my old pal, Ann, knew.

Nothing serious, just lunch, once in a while, I promised myself. I thought he was fascinated by my life and wanted to bring me to further adventures but was smart enough to cloak his aims in puritan terms.

The day I met with the superiors to sign my final papers, the boyfriend came to the convent area with me. I parked my rattle-trap of a car about a block away and ordered him to wait there inside my car. The Superior was warm and solicitous. She even gave me a sisterly embrace. After I signed the multiple papers, she opened a skinny wallet, and pulled out a hundred dollar bill like my father gave to Mother Josepha when I started my long journey to becoming a nun. I could see my car out of the corner of my eye, and sent my boyfriend telegraphic messages to not open the car door. Finally, the goodbyes were over. One last hug, one last, "God bless you." It was over.

I walked sedately down the little cement walkway. The convent door clicked shut behind me. Suddenly, I began running down the street toward my car. I could hear the motor revving up. Vroom! Vroom!

I jumped into the car on the driver's side. My hundred dollar bill was in a hidden pocket in my jacket. I was grinning. I was laughing. I was singing. I was praying out loud.

I pulled the car over to a side street and kissed my startled boyfriend over and over in a most un-nunly fashion. In between the kisses, I told him about the hundred dollar bill. I asked him to do the driving.

I wanted to go to a fancy restaurant together. I wanted to eat lobster and drink champagne with him.

I started my new life that day madly, wildly, and unforgettably.

I never looked back.

CPSIA information can be obtained
at www.ICGtesting.com
Printed in the USA
BVHW082001220121
598424BV00010B/1132